There's Got to Be an Easier Way to Run a Restaurant

How to Have a Successful Company ... AND A LIFE!

BILL MARVIN

Hospitality Masters Press
PO Box 280 • Gig Harbor, WA 98335

ClickArt by T/Maker

Library of Congress Control Number: 2015914549

ISBN 978-1-893864-06-1

ATTENTION ASSOCIATIONS AND MULTI-UNIT OPERATORS:
Quantity discounts are available on bulk purchases of this book for premiums, sales promotions, educational purposes or fund raising. Custom imprinting or book excerpts can also be created to fit specific needs.

For more information, please contact our Special Sales Department
Hospitality Masters Press, PO Box 280, Gig Harbor, WA 98335
(800) 767-1055, e-mail: info@hospitalitymasterspress.com
Outside the US and Canada, phone (253) 858-9255

There's Got to Be an Easier Way to Run a Restaurant
How to Have a Successful Company ... and a Life!

CONTENTS

Part 1
INTRODUCTION

Preface to the Revised Edition 3
1. Help Wanted 5
2. How to Read this Book 8
3. Of Coaches and Cops 11

Part 2
OUT OF THE WEEDS

4. Lost in the Weeds 17
5. Life on the Beach 21
6. Out of the Weeds 24

Part 3
A FRESH LOOK AT MANAGEMENT

7. Leadership and Management 29
8. The Leader as a Compass 31
9. A Short Lesson in Leadership 32
10. The Power of the Vision 33
11. The Power of Impersonal Purpose 35
12. The Power of the Quiet Mind 37
13. Tell Your Story 39
14. Get the Herd Moving 40
15. Seek Alignment, Not Agreement 42
16. Be in Alignment With Your Guests 43
17. Chris the Dishwasher 44
18. Your Real Job 47
19. The Power of Presence 50
20. Motivation 55
21. Climate 58
22. The Day From Hell 61
23. Listening 67
24. The Benefit of the Doubt 69
25. Serve Your Staff 70
26. Value and Respect Your Staff 71
27. Value a Free and Clear Mind 72
28. Support Your Staff 74
29. Respect the Power of the Climate 75

30. Set a Personal Example 77
31. What's Your Problem? 78
32. Problem Solving 80
33. Finding Solutions 82
34. Give Your Job Away 84
35. Taking Ownership 85
36. How Rules Are Made 89
37. Sound Familiar? 91
38. Lazy People 93
39. Moving the Company 94
40. Columbo Management 98
41. Lists 102
42. Stress 105
43. Warning Signs 108
44. Pre-Determined Ideas 109
45. Start to Notice 112
46. Don't Compete, Excel 114
47. Tone of Voice 116

Part 4
YEAH, BUT ...

48. Getting Acclimated 121
49. Out to Lunch 122
50. Non-Compliance 124
51. Freeing up the Future 128
52. Reaching Agreement 131

Part 5
WHERE TO FROM HERE?

53. The Daily Question 137
54. Fix the System, Not the People 140
55. Making it Safe 143
56. Dumb as Dirt 145
57. A Meeting of the Minds 146
58. The Meeting Mindset 148
59. Staff Meetings Step by Step 149
60. Monitor Your Meetings 152
61. Breaking Old Habits 155
62. Closing Comments 158

APPENDIX

About the Author 163
Management Resources 164
How to Become the Restaurant of Choice 167
Re-Thinking Restaurants 168

Part 1

Introduction

"We are on the verge of the new age, a whole new world. Mankind's consciousness, our mutual awareness, is going to make a quantum leap.
Everything will change. You will never be the same.
All this will happen just as soon as you're ready."

– Paul Williams, Das Energi

Preface to the Revised Edition

This book is about the understandings that changed my life, personally and professionally. In truth, I suspect they actually *saved* my life.

If I'd continued working the 80+ hour weeks that had become my routine in the foodservice business, I'd likely have been laid to rest long before now. I would certainly have had a far tougher life and missed half the adventures that have made this journey interesting.

I was struck by the elegant simplicity of these principles in 1979 and life as I'd come to know it changed immediately. But it took another twenty years before I had the words to be able to share them with others.

Our industry desperately needs to discover these insights. Collectively, we've learned how to do things the hard way, but it you don't know of any other way to do it, you just think it's hard. Like any information with the ability to change life for the better, I feel duty-bound to pass along what I've learned. You may get it and you may not, but to withhold something so simple and so powerful would be irresponsible.

In this updated edition, I've included more amplifying material and revised much of my original language to (hopefully) more effectively convey what can only be imperfectly expressed in writing.

This book is not about the "stuff" that's in it, it's about the larger picture the content is pointing toward. When you catch a glimpse of that, when you're struck by the simple elegance of it, life as you know it will painlessly – almost magically – change for the better.

This isn't a "how to" manual. Don't adopt anything I say as a technique. Rather, listen to the words as you might listen to music. Reflect on the notions and validate them from your own experience. Clear your mind and open yourself to fresh possibilities. The rest happens automatically. It's just that easy.

Bill Marvin
The Restaurant Doctor^{SM}
Gig Harbor, Washington

"There is more to life than increasing its speed"
– Mahatma Gandhi

1
Help Wanted

If you ran an honest ad for your job, would it look anything like this?

MANAGER WANTED

Must be willing to: sell soul to the company, work 70-80 hours a week for little more than minimum wage, miss children's growing up, lose marriage, start drinking heavily, live with stress and die of a coronary at age 57.

Do you think your phone would be ringing off the hook with eager applicants? Of course not ... and unless this is your idea of a good time, you don't have to put up with this sort of life, either.

Easy to say, perhaps, but what else can you do?

My professional background is in the restaurant business. I got my first job washing dishes (by hand!) when I was 14 and have been in and around the business ever since as an hourly worker, manager, owner and consultant. The examples throughout this book are necessarily be from that experience ... although I think you'd easily find similar situations in almost any business enterprise.

Foodservice is a labor-intensive industry with a well-deserved reputation for demanding incredibly long hours from its managers.

I graduated from one of the country's premier hospitality programs, yet even in school – as in every foodservice job I held – I was taught this is a killer business where you needed to work 18 hours a day, eight days a week. I was told if I wasn't willing to make that kind of time commitment, I should pursue another career path.

I never questioned this bit of insanity. I suspect most businesses have a similar myth passed down from one manager to the next. You may have bought into an idea like this, too. The problem is that it's just not true.

The Cost of Misunderstanding

The price we pay for this lack of understanding is staggering. It shows up in the form of lower profits, reduced productivity, burnout, turnover, broken marriages, substance abuse and a crushing level of stress.

The sad truth is that a majority of the problems most managers deal with day after day are not inherent problems of the restaurant business but rather very predictable symptoms of their level of understanding (or lack of same) about people, and their ingrained notions of what it takes to be an effective manager.

Even as I was working myself to death (120 hours a week in one job!), I couldn't help but feel there just **had** to be an easier way to get the results I wanted. I've always been a hard worker but I'm not a masochist, so I started looking for other approaches that might be more effective.

A New Model

Perhaps because I was actively looking for a better way, I crossed paths with folks doing breakthrough work, primarily in the mental health field, gaining a fresh understanding of how individuals really function. They were seeing results in weeks that conventional therapy had not been able to achieve in years. It seemed like magic.

I immediately saw how the principles could apply to hospitality operations and suddenly I understood what I was trying to do in a different and much simpler way. As soon as I saw that bigger picture, I was suddenly off the old management treadmill.

The human part of my work became effortless and the difference in my effectiveness was earthshaking! The answer seemed so obvious, I wondered why nobody had ever taught me this.

Remember Columbus

It's easy to think, "In your dreams. It just can't that easy." If you feel that way, I'll remind you that in 1491, the world was flat! Everybody knew the world was flat – it was a fact of life, yet just a year later, it was impossible to hold that view. The world didn't change, only the way we all thought about it was different.

That little voice in your head that says, "There's GOT to be an easier way to do this," is right.

Once your understanding shifts and you start to see things from a different perspective, your life, both professionally and personally, changes forever. Really.

A Blinding Flash of the Obvious
You already have the answers but you just don't see them yet because they're not where you're used to looking. The shift comes when you recognize a few common sense truths that have been right in front of you all along but which, because of the way you were trained to think, you never noticed before.

This book examines a few of the principles that can help you make this shift for yourself ... if you have the courage to let your life be easier.

Buckle up and let's get started!

2
How to Read this Book

Because I write like I talk, my wording tends to be more chatty and informal. I hope that makes the material more user-friendly and easier to follow. I've also scattered a few cartoons around to give your eyes a break from endless seas of text.

Please don't let the casual presentation cause you to take these notions less seriously. Information doesn't have to be dull to be life-changing.

The shift to a new frame of reference is an inside-out learning process. Unfortunately, our education system doesn't teach us much about how to do that, so let me explain.

Outside-In Learning

For the most part, our model of education is outside-in – it's based on "stuff." (I'm the teacher and I know the stuff. You're a dummy because you don't know the stuff. So I'll tell you about the stuff, you write it all down and then we'll have a quiz. If you can spit back enough stuff, you'll get a good grade and we'll call you educated!)

I don't mean to knock the "stuff" – it's better to know it than to not know it. Knowledge is more powerful than ignorance. But did you ever have a course you took – maybe even one you got a good grade in – that you can't remember a thing about anymore?

The problem with knowledge is that you only have it as long as you remember it. The mental shift that will change your personal and professional life isn't about more information or finding new tools for your tool belt. It results from seeing things from a different frame of reference. Understanding is more powerful than knowledge.

Inside-Out Learning

When you learn from the inside out, you reach your own insights rather than adopt someone else's views.

For example, I could describe – perhaps even eloquently – the view from my deck. I could talk about Puget Sound, Vashon Island, Mt. Rainier, the ferries and such. Perhaps I could even do it well enough that you'd start to have a sense of what it must be like.

However, you'd find it hard to describe the view to another person with any degree of certainty because you'd only have my words to go on. The view would be a concept, not a personal reality.

But come to my house, stand on the deck, and immediately it's **your** view. You'd have your own images and could convey your sense of the view as well (or maybe even better) than I might. In other words, once you'd seen it, we'd both own the view.

Personally, I'd rather get better at giving directions to the house than try to improve my ability to describe the view. This is what inside-out learning is like ... and what this book is all about.

Here are a few suggestions on how to facilitate this inside-out process of self-learning using this book:

Avoid Judgment

Judgment is when you take new information, bounce it off old information and say, "I like this, I don't like that. I agree or I don't agree. Oh, that's what Covey meant when he said ..." All this does is keep you stuck in old thinking, it won't help you grow. Stop it.

Read Lightly

You have to read a bit differently, too. We've been taught to study the content, to memorize key points of a text in preparation for "the quiz." That won't help you. You need to read lightly. Get the gist of what I'm pointing toward. Grasp the spirit behind the words. Try to see the view rather than memorize its description.

The message you're looking for is in the *feeling* behind the words, not in the words themselves.

Be Curious

Roll these ideas around in your brain and reflect on how they might be applied. Look for possibilities. Don't try to "make sense" of anything. Just sit with it awhile and see if it starts to fit. It's OK to feel a bit lost – to not "get it" immediately. Learning to become comfortable in the unknown is the first step to creative insight.

Validate from Your Own Experience

Perhaps the strongest idea is to reflect on your personal dealings with people and see if, in fact, these principles directly match with your own experience of what actually works and what doesn't.

One Final Suggestion

Human beings seem to like complex constructions. We love things like seven habits of highly effective bartenders or thirty-seven steps to great service. Elaborate theories can be seductive "mind candy." They are well-intentioned, but in the end, they're just more "stuff" to remember.

Don't be too clever for your own good. Resist the urge to make these principles into something complicated. The answer you seek is far easier than that. The answer you seek is hiding in plain sight. If it seems elusive, it's only because of its simplicity and common sense.

The first time through, the ideas in this book may strike you as things you already know. But if you're willing to keep your mind open and re-visit the material a few times, each time through, the ideas will touch you at a deeper and deeper level.

Somewhere in this process it will suddenly all fall into place for you. You'll be struck by exciting insights you missed completely in the first few passes – and that will make all the difference!

Trust me on this.

3
Of Coaches and Cops

No matter what the specific symptoms, people are the common denominators in all business issues. People cause all the problems and it's people who must ultimately be part of any lasting solutions.

We all say ours is a "people business," but who ever really taught us about people? I suspect most folks become supervisors by decree: "You've been here the longest (you've got a degree, your family owns the place, or whatever) so you're the new supervisor. Go out there and supervise."

In truth, few (if any) managers get any real training in what makes people tick. The closest I came was a psychology course in high school where we talked about paranoid schizophrenics and manic-depressives, but never about normal people!

Even my college management courses were a lot closer to advanced manipulation than anything else! Without a deeper understanding to fall back on, I learned to manage by following the model set by my previous managers, most of whom would be in jail if they tried to operate today like they operated back then!

The Cop Mentality
Odds are your model of management came from former managers who grew up with a cop mentality. "Find things that are wrong and fix them" usually was (and typically still is) the order of the day for a management cop.

This model of supervision is more like law enforcement than enlightened leadership, but that's what they taught us because that was just the way things were done. It was all they knew. But was it effective?

Cops look for problems. They tend to see others as crooks who must be kept under control at all times. Cop mentality believes you can compel your staff to deliver quality service and that you can motivate them effectively with fear.

The idea that "the floggings will continue until morale improves" makes sense to a cop. Following the cop model, many people try to force their staff to perform and expect that it'll work.

There's no question that you can get results this way ... but what results? And at what price?

One of my consulting clients once admitted, "By any standard, we've been successful. We have been profitable since the day we opened and we're the leading restaurants in the markets we serve. But the price we've paid has been staggering. Our wake is littered with bodies!"

There was a time when it seemed like we had disposable labor, when we could treat people any way we wanted because there was a line of good applicants at the door looking for work. Perhaps we could get away with it then, but the cop mentality is seldom effective in the long run because it's an external force and doesn't properly consider the human factors.

The cop mentality creates organizations that don't work – an unfortunate result that many erroneously ascribe to the poor quality of today's workers rather than to the inherent unworkability of the model. However, if you thrive on stress and want to spend the rest of your life looking for the dark side and fighting fires, the cop style of management will certainly produce that result!

The Coaching Mentality
In the age of service (and we *are* in the age of service if you didn't notice), a more appropriate management style is coaching.

Coaches look for strengths. Coaches look at the talent they have to work with and devise a game plan to win with the skills available on the team. Coaches realize that the talent resides in the players and if the players fail to achieve *their* full potential, the team will never reach *its* full potential.

Coaches know that motivation is found internally, not externally. The best coaches don't try to force people to do anything they don't want to do or are incapable of doing.

Like farmers, coaches realize that while contented cows may not necessarily give more milk, they don't kick the bucket over as often and are a lot easier to live with!

Donald I. Smith, former football coach, hospitality industry leader and Professor Emeritus at Washington State University has always taught that the coach makes the difference.

Here are some of his ideas on coaches and coaching that are worth considering:

"Great coaches are first noticed by their uncanny ability to produce championship teams. However, to be called 'coach,' a leader must be measured by more than balance sheets, battles won or lifetime win-loss records.

"Great coaches have one more gift. They change the lives of those they touch. Great coaches are measured by the number of success stories they leave in their wake.

For once they give their players a taste of sweet success, they will have more. They leave behind a legacy of winning which becomes a lifetime habit. The players ultimately become champions of the coach's values, beliefs and passions for the rest of their lives."

When you start to see yourself as a coach, your approach changes. The way you measure personal success shifts from the number of problems you've solved and moves in the direction of tracking the number of wins your staff is enjoying.

To improve your coaching skills, develop your ability to ask the right questions. Great coaches ask insightful, probing questions that cause their players to think ... and find their own answers.

It's hard to get into trouble if you're either asking or answering questions. It's only when you make unsolicited statements (preaching or lecturing) that you tread on dangerous ground.

Making the Shift
While you may have heard these cop/coach notions before, just grasping the concept intellectually won't change anything. Your organization isn't likely to change until your **thinking** actually shifts.

For example, even though you may know that trust is an important element for the new workforce, you can't trust people as a technique. You'll only trust people when you truly see them as trustworthy. The shift of perspective is everything.

Do you get that the problems "out there" are only symptoms of how you are thinking "in here?"

The purpose of this book is to help you see that, to give you some ideas on how to clean up your internal state and help you discover a fresh frame of reference.

Our goal is to arrive at that "aha" moment where you slap your head and say, "Wow! I never looked at things quite like *that* before!"

Once you truly see a bigger picture and are moved by the simplicity and common sense of what you see, you will effortlessly and painlessly make the leap to this new understanding. You'll be out of the weeds and onto the beach ... forever!

Like most things that are simple, this new model isn't always an easy picture to see at first, but I promise it will be worth whatever it takes for you to move into this new reality.

Be curious, keep an open mind, relax and be patient. All the answers you seek will reveal themselves to you when you least expect them.

Part 2

Out of the Weeds

"Just because a blind man can't see the heavens,
doesn't mean the stars don't exist"
— Sydney Banks

4
Lost in the Weeds

For many managers and owners, operating a business is a lot like being lost in the jungle. In the restaurant industry we'd talk about being lost in the weeds! When this is what your life is like, you show up every day and cut weeds, trying to keep a clear space to operate.

The work is hot, you get tired and sweaty, your back aches, the bugs bite and you have to keep an eye out for snakes. Still, you can't stop cutting for long because the weeds grow back quickly whenever you take a break.

Does this sound familiar? In the world of weeds, people are always on the lookout for better ways to cut.

Breakthroughs are improved cutting techniques ("keep your elbow straight and swing from the shoulder ..."). There's endless debate about cutting implements ("curved blades are better than straight blades ..."). There are chain saw champions, napalm nuts, poison promoters and so forth – each arguing for a new and better way to cut weeds.

People make careers of studying different weeds, learning their technical names and researching their growth patterns. There are dozens of weed management programs, each with its supporters and detractors.

Consultants get wealthy showing people new and different ways to hack away at their particular set of weeds, but no matter how efficient you get at it, you're still in the weed-cutting business.

Occasionally you may hear some "crazy" person suggest weed-cutting is unnecessary. This loony may even be so bold to suggest there's a world without weeds. Madness! So you continue to hack away, dismissing him as a crackpot who obviously doesn't have a grasp of "reality," all the while cursing the weeds.

You know weed-cutting is backbreaking work but it's the only world you know. With some pride, you may even brag that you're starting to know the weeds much better and are developing a really good cutting stroke!

You're spurred on by the naive belief that if you only continue to apply yourself diligently to the task, eventually you'll get ahead of the weeds, and everything will be perfect. What are you pretending not to know?

The truth is that nothing much ever changes in the world of weeds. If enhanced cutting skills could yield the happy, productive team you dream about, you'd already be seeing that sort of result.

A manager once told me he knew that what he was doing didn't work, but he didn't want to consider alternatives because he was finally getting really good at it! How about you?

Are you getting better and better at things that don't work?

Albert Einstein once observed that you can't solve a problem on the level at which it was created. In other words, the thinking that got you *into* a problem isn't likely to get you *out* of that problem!

To apply this to my analogy here, if you ever want to get out of the weed-cutting business, you first have to see a bigger picture. You have to climb a tree.

Actually, you must first recognize there is even such a thing **as** a tree. In the world of weeds, trees just look like particularly nasty weeds!

When you go up a tree a bit – when you can view your world from a wider perspective – you suddenly see that the weeds only grow in the small area immediately around you. Just on the other side of your weed patch is a beach with a little bar. Who knew?

Once you see the true lay of the land, your own innate common sense will take over. You'll clearly see you could just as easily be sitting in the sun with a frosty beverage. All you have to do is choose to walk out of the weed patch ... and why wouldn't you do it?

The "crazy folks" were right – you never had to cut weeds in the first place ... but you couldn't see that for yourself until you allowed your perspective to expand. You were lost and didn't even know it.

This book is about helping you to move out of the weeds and onto the beach.

Even as our hero relaxes on the shore with an adult beverage, there are people back in the weeds hacking away and thinking to themselves, "There's GOT to be more to life than this!"

(And if he tried to tell them about the beach, they'd call him a mad man who'd lost his grip on "reality" and doesn't understand what it takes to succeed in the business!)

Who are really the crazy ones?

5
Life on the Beach

You know about living in the weeds. What's it like to live on the beach? To help you understand why you might want to make the shift, here are some comments from one executive who saw a different picture.

The words are those of the CEO of a Midwest advertising company. In the early 80's, the company's former owners did what a lot of people did in the early 80's – they leveraged the company, took the money and ran, leaving the organization with an incredible debt.

They still had healthy sales, but were barely showing a profit.

A week after he took over as the new CEO, the bank phoned to say they were going to call the company's loans! "Give us the money back." He swallowed hard and said, "give me six months."

(He confessed that he didn't know at the time what he was going to *do* in those six months, but he knew he needed time to do something!)

He got in touch with the folks who were instrumental in pointing me in the direction I'm talking with you about. He applied what he learned and everything changed.

Rather than go into the details of what he did, how he did it or how the company's financial picture changed (I don't have that info anyway!), perhaps this will convey the impact of his shift of understanding:

A year later, he said he was getting phone calls from the same banker saying, "We have a couple of problem companies in our portfolio. If we loaned you the money, would you buy them?"

Now *that's* a serious turnaround!

This is the way he described his "new" organization:

Imagine a work place where the environment is calm, yet people are intensely involved in work activities.

Imagine business meetings so enjoyable and productive that people leave more energized than when they arrived.

Imagine managers making decisions based on reflection rather than from fear or by knee jerk reaction to circumstances.

Imagine a work force so resilient that disruptive factors like disappointment and change have but a very temporary effect.

Imagine the energy so often wasted dealing with interpersonal and individual stress being put, instead, into the work itself.

Imagine an environment where there's no concern about motivating people with incentives or pressure since people are generally happy and productive.

Imagine morale at such a high level that staff and managers arrive home from work in a state of mind that actually increases the well-being of the people in their lives, rather than detracting from it.

Imagine an organization that has trust and confidence in its staff, allowing them to be responsible for their own thinking.

Imagine a happy, healthy and productive group of men and women who actualize levels of ability and service which they did not even know they were capable of.

Imagine taking your company to a higher level than you ever dreamed possible by accessing the fundamental innate intelligence of your staff.

How does that sound? If this was honestly an accurate description of the way your company operated ...

What do you think would be happening for you in the market?

What do you think it would be like for guests to patronize you?

What do you think it would be like to work in your operation?

From my own experience, I can assure you his description is not only extremely accurate, but it's the way things are **supposed** to be. As idealistic as it may sound, with an enlightened leader, all organizations are capable of functioning this way – it's hardwired into human nature.

The extent to which you are **not** seeing behavior like this in your company is merely the extent to which your own understanding (or lack of it) is getting in the way.

6
Out of the Weeds

If you find management to be a struggle, the problem most likely lies in your thinking about what it takes to run your company, your ideas about what you're supposed to be as a manager and your understanding of what makes people tick.

The first step to get from the weeds to the beach is a willingness to open yourself to the notion that there are possibilities beyond your current level of understanding.

Some suggest there are three possible types of information: the things you know that you know, the things you know that you don't know and the things you don't know that you don't know.

In other words, we all have blind spots, we just don't know where they are ... which, of course, is what makes them blind spots!

You can't reach the beach until you're willing to shine a light into your blind spots. When you can drop judgements and personal ego long enough to open yourself to new possibilities and insights, you will be amazed at what you'll suddenly discover.

The second step toward a weed-free life is to realize that you don't quite know how to get there from where you are now.

If you did, you wouldn't be working so hard or feeling so stressed and you certainly wouldn't be dealing with the types of problems you're dealing with now. The humility required to honestly admit that you don't have a clue is a major aid to finally seeing the path toward an easier life.

While all this may sound too good to be true, I promise that the beach exists and that you **can** get there. Making the shift involves deepening your understanding of people, not building your repertoire of techniques.

You're looking for what some describe as a blinding flash of the obvious ... and that comes from personal insight rather than from linear (reasoned) thinking.

There's that inside-out learning again!

"What we (and other like-minded folks around the country) are doing is creating a new, more constructive, sustainable way to work."

– Ari Weinzweig, Zingerman's

Part 3

A Fresh Look at Management

"Never doubt that a small group of thoughtful, concerned citizens can change world. Indeed it is the only thing that ever has."

– Margaret Mead

7
Leadership and Management

The terms leader and manager are often used interchangeably but they are really very different skill sets.

A common distinction is that managers are concerned with doing things right and leaders are focused on doing the right things ... but perhaps an even more powerful differentiation is that managers have subordinates while leaders have followers.

Successful organizations need both managers and leaders, of course, and many people wear both hats, particularly in small businesses. My personal experience is that the more effective the leadership, the less actual management is required to get things done.

Since leadership is the most critical – and elusive – of the two roles, that is my immediate focus ... but it also presents a few challenges.

The question usually asked is, "What do I have to do to be a better leader?" It's a fair question ... but unfortunately, it's the wrong one.

I suspect people look for specific actions to take because their early career development likely revolved around the things they learned to do. Those skills are good, but here's the rub: **Doing** is primarily the realm of management where leadership is more about **Being**.

Another way to look at it is that in management, the things you do come first after which you get to **be** something (a more efficient line cook, a profitable restaurant, etc.)

In contrast, leadership comes before anything is done. The leader champions a compelling vision that excites the organization, and the necessary activities, whatever they may be, follow naturally from that.

If you were hoping for a checklist of what you must do to be a good leader, I can't help you. That's just not the way leadership works. However, I *can* help you see what you must bring to the party – how you must *be* – to be a good leader.

If you can do that, you'll inspire a following and collectively, the group will always know what to do next.

In his book, *Corporate Culture*, Allen Kennedy wryly suggests that the basic challenge of leadership is to get the whole herd moving roughly west! In my seminars, I often use this line. It's always good for a chuckle ... but it's also a real-world metaphor.

It speaks to the two biggest roles that leaders have: The first and perhaps largest challenge, is determining which way is west – which direction the company should be headed. The essential second task is getting the herd moving in that direction.

8

The Leader as a Compass

Great leaders seem to have an innate sense of where they're going. Once they decide they want to head west, they always know where west is.

They effectively become a compass that unerringly keeps the efforts and energy of the company focused in the right direction regardless of outside conditions.

This clarity of direction comes from a clear vision – a dream or a purpose if you will – of a larger possibility for the company. Without that vision, it's easy to get lost in complexity.

Like a small boat in a storm, those without a vision are tossed about on a chaotic sea of swirling problems and pressures, changing direction depending on the prevailing winds and generally behaving more like a weather vane than a compass.

The inevitable result of this lack of direction is that everyone in the organization becomes lost, stressed, discouraged and unproductive. Many will even jump ship rather than continue to work in such chaos.

Without the steadying effect of a clear vision, would-be leaders tend to get confused and "freeze up" in a crisis. They either try to enforce an arbitrary set of rules to preserve their illusion of control (micro-manage) or simply disappear from the scene.

9
A Short Lesson in Leadership

The ten-part HBO mini-series "Band of Brothers" presented the true story of a company of paratroopers in World War II, from the D-Day invasion to the end of the war.

One character was Lt. Norman Dyke, a company commander. When the company was under fire, he either stayed in his foxhole or disappeared on "essential errands" to battalion headquarters, leaving his First Sergeant in charge.

The First Sergeant described Lt. Dyke as an "empty uniform" – physically present, at least some of the time, but totally lacking in leadership.

The narrator summed it up nicely in two sentences when he said, "**Lt. Dyke is not a bad leader because he makes bad decisions. He is a bad leader because he makes NO decisions.**"

This got me thinking about bad leaders I've known. When the operation was getting slammed, the toilets backed up or emergencies arose, they either found compelling work that had to be done in the office, or headed off on "essential errands" to the bank or the restaurant supply store or anywhere that would get them out of the place.

I may be preaching to the choir here, but the job of a leader is to lead ... and that can't be done from the rear.

A leader must be in front of the troops when they need leadership – to assess the situation, assign tasks, answer questions, provide assurance and keep them moving in the right direction.

A leader lets the company know they're in good hands so they can focus on the tasks of the moment. The leader makes decisions when they need to be made and shows no fear. It's less important that all the decisions are 100% correct or that the leader is unafraid.

Where are you when the bullets start flying?

10
The Power of the Vision

Vision is another one of those buzzwords that gets abused and misinterpreted to the point where it often loses its meaning. But really a vision is simply your mental image of how things could (or should) be in a way that has never been seen before – a dream of a potential future beyond anything previously imagined.

A vision is not a goal. Goals are just incremental steps toward the greater possibility represented by the dream of the leader. If the company doesn't have a vision – a larger purpose – it doesn't really need a leader. Without a leader moving the group to new pastures, day-to-day life can sink into the drudgery of same old-same old.

A vision won't come from asking how to do a better job of what you're already doing. It comes from reflecting on larger questions like "Are we doing the right things?" and "What larger contribution could we make to the world?"

True visions always deal with the unknown and they're rare. If your "vision" comes too quickly, if you have many of them or if you're sure you know what needs to be done do bring your vision into being, It's either too small or you don't have a true vision.

Most likely you're just seeing incremental steps toward a larger, as yet undefined, possibility. Stay with it. You don't exactly know what you're searching for but you'll recognize it when it finds you.

When it reveals itself, a true vision can scare you with its audacity. It will be huge and transformational – something that's never been done before because nobody every thought it was possible. You'll feel totally inadequate to take it on and you'll be clueless as to how to make it happen. (Sound like fun, yet?)

The good news is that it will also be compelling. It won't leave you alone. The very fact that it's "impossible" will be incredibly exciting and that will draw others who want to be part of helping it happen.

Here's the best part: all it really takes to turn a vision into reality is your own clarity, some focused action and a little time. That may sound a bit metaphysical – perhaps it is – but everything man has created in this physical world started as just somebody's "crazy idea."

Someone had a vision of a different future and said, "You know, we could ..." Others became excited by the possibility, stepped up to aid the cause and together these pioneers did what needed to be done to bring the idea to reality.

I've seen examples of this phenomenon in my lifetime. In the early 60s, President John Kennedy said in a speech that before the end of the decade, the US should have the goal to put a man on the moon and return him safely to earth.

It wasn't just that nobody at the time had a clue as to how to do that – nobody knew if that was even possible. It was well beyond any of the technology of the day.

But mundane "realities" will never stop a truly great vision and Kennedy's vision was so big and so impossible that it got people excited.

Experts from all disciplines were drawn to the task and came together around this shared dream. Energized by the clarity and challenge of the vision, they figured out what had to be figured out, invented what needed to be invented and learned what nobody ever had to learn before.

On July 20, 1969, Apollo 11 landed on the moon. On July 21, Neil Armstrong stepped onto the moon's surface. On July 24 the Lunar Module safely landed in the Pacific Ocean ... and Kennedy's "impossible" vision was realized, right on schedule.

11
The Power of Impersonal Purpose

Nobody gets up in the morning with a burning urge to give you money. To keep your passion alive and make a meaningful contribution to the community, you must play a larger game than just trying to sell as many meals (or t-shirts, insurance policies, etc.) as possible.

No matter how many you sell, your focus is still on what's in it for you and that's playing a small game. A leader needs followers drawn by the chance to make a difference. Making money for somebody else is just a job. Nobody's going to get that excited about it.

Even if it doesn't change what you're doing, a larger purpose will change the way people feel about what their work. This phenomenon is clearly illustrated by a story you've probably heard in some version before.

Variations of this tale have been told for thousands of years. The oldest stories survive because they contain a deeper truth that continues to resonate with successive generations of listeners. Here is the essence of the message:

A traveler came upon a group of three stonemasons. Each was hard at work chipping away at blocks of marble. The traveler asked each man what he was doing. The first said, "I'm chipping a block of marble." The second said, "I'm preparing a foundation." The third said, "I'm building a cathedral."

True power and liberation will naturally follow when you make a passionate personal commitment to a large compelling vision – an impersonal goal – where the focus is not on what you DO or what's in it for you, but on the greater good others derive from your doing it.

You still must execute well and make a profit, of course – I'm not talking about becoming a charity. To be sustainable and deliver on your vision, you must continue to be a viable business.

But when your focus is on the larger good created by what you do (rather than by whatever gain is in it for you personally), not only will you have more fun, do a better job and make more money, but people will come out of the woodwork to help you do it.

You will attract followers ... and you'll be a leader.

Think about it: Would you rather be in the business of selling pizzas or would you prefer to be all about bringing friends and families together over a shared meal and enriching their lives with the experience of exceptional hospitality?

Either way you'll prepare and serve pizza, but ...

which game sounds more fulfilling for you and your crew?

which approach is likely to be more appealing to potential customers?

which model is more likely to keep your passion engaged over time?

which game is apt to produce higher pizza sales in the long run?

I rest my case.

You aren't truly a leader unless you have followers and you won't have any followers unless you're taking them somewhere they can't get to on their own. You need a clear sense of direction toward a larger, impersonal purpose to draw them to you.

About now you may be asking how you get in touch with your vision in the first place. Where do visions come from? How do you find them?

I'm glad you asked.

12
The Power of the Quiet Mind

Were you ever working on a tough problem and getting absolutely nowhere ... making pro and con lists, running "what if" scenarios in your mind, your nostrils filled with the smell of burning brain cells ... and still coming up empty?

Then suddenly you had an insight – a blinding flash of the obvious – and the answer that magically appeared was absolutely spot on? Has that ever happened to you? I think that sort of breakthrough has happened for everyone at one time or another.

Would I be safe to guess that the insight didn't come in the middle of working on the problem?

It might come as you were just falling asleep ... or just waking up ... or in the shower ... or playing with the kids ... or on the golf course. For me, when I totally give up on finding an answer to my problem, the solution seems to pop up and slap me in the head.

Insights don't result from any sort of problem-solving activity. Rather they arise from the receptive environment created by reducing the chatter in your head and quieting your mind to a point where you can recognize the gift when it appears.

When your mind quiets down, you tap into a flow of wisdom that's far deeper than anything you can access consciously. The quiet mind is the realm of insight and that's where you must go to see a larger picture.

That's where you get a sense of what you want to be when you grow up. That's where you discover a vision of exciting outcomes that aren't there now but could be ... should be ... must be.

It reminds me of the restaurant phrase, "Slow down, you'll go faster." I can't adequately explain what that means. When you get it, you'll know.

Getting clear on your purpose takes reflection, not struggle, but it won't happen overnight ... which is probably why most independent operators think they're just too busy to do it.

Yes, it takes time to get it right, but the process of reaching clarity will ultimately save more time (and make you more money) than anything else you can do.

When you truly grasp what you're on the planet to accomplish, it provides a standard against which you can evaluate every decision you make and every action you consider as you move forward.

A clear, impersonal purpose is incredibly compelling. It gives you energy and a reason to get up in the morning and go to work each day. It draws followers to your cause. Perhaps best of all, it changes the way your team feels about what they are doing.

They stop simply chipping rocks and become engaged in building your cathedral ... together.

I can't tell you what your purpose is or should be. One size doesn't fit all. But the discovery process is painless.

First, drop distractions, quiet your mind and slow down to the speed of life. Then reflect on the needs in your community. If you could wave a magic wand, what "impossible dream" would transform the quality of life for everyone in your neighborhood?

There's nothing to figure out – just stay calm and let something strike you. It's like standing beside a river watching ideas float by like leaves in the current. When you notice something that catches your imagination, pluck it out and see if it grows on you.

Discovering your purpose can be an exercise in patience. You can't rush the process – you'll see it when you're ready for it – but "the vision thing" is tremendously exciting, professionally essential and the only job in the company you can't delegate to someone else.

It is the true work of a leader.

13
Tell Your Story

With your vision clearly in mind, the next step is to craft your Great Story – the inspiring tale of what you envision, why it is needed, who will be profoundly affected by it and how it will change their lives.

Paint it with your passion and color it with your commitment, knowing that you are the perfect person – the only person – who can bring this impossible mission to a successful conclusion.

The people of the world are hungry for a great story of a great calling, one that makes them think of possibilities, one that touches their hearts with its clarity, simplicity and magnitude.

The world has been waiting for you to do this and your story, passionately told, will draw followers to your cause.

Your story becomes richer and more refined the more you share it. The tale articulates your vision and allows others to see a role for themselves in a more noble venture. Eventually, fulfilling your vision becomes their crusade as well.

14
Get the Herd Moving

The best part of all this is that when you have a clear vision, make a unshakeable commitment to see it through, and tell your story with passion to enough people, it won't take much else to get the herd moving in the right direction.

At that point, your biggest concern will be just to stay ahead of the mob and avoid being trampled as they all charge off ... toward the west ... filled with their own passion and a shared sense of purpose.

Once the herd is moving, your primary role as the leader is to be the protector of the dream. You are the compass that keeps the herd on the right trail, but you must be impeccable in your pursuit of the dream and continually keep an eye out for strays.

Within the parameter of "roughly west" you will have people headed straight west at a dead run and you'll have others who seem to be milling around. But if the overall movement is roughly west, you're OK.

Some days you'll move faster than others, but in the real world, any motion in the right direction is a good thing.

Occasionally you'll see someone wandering off to the north. Now north is a good direction; there's nothing wrong with north, it's just not the direction your herd is headed.

When you find a northbound person in your westbound herd, you need to find out if they're just disoriented or if they're truly northbound.

If they're lost, offer a little course correction and point them back toward the west. If they are truly northbound, put them in touch with a north-bound organization. It will work out better for everyone!

There's a time for each of us to head off in our own direction. Your job as an effective leader is not to fight that urge, merely to channel it in an appropriate manner.

For example, hockey legend Wayne Gretzky is a world class athlete, but if you're going to play basketball, he'll either have to lose the skates ... or go next door to the ice rink where they'll be excited to see him!

If you have the courage to let go of the myth that you can somehow force everyone to work as a team, and instead be content to monitor the direction the herd is moving and make course corrections as necessary, the day-to-day work seems to flow more easily!

15
Seek Alignment, Not Agreement

The most powerful force on earth is a shared vision. As the leader, you are the chief dreamer, resident compass and traffic director. It's not realistic – or necessary – that everyone agrees on the way every task is performed. In fact, it hardly ever happens.

The important thing is not that everyone is in agreement but that they're all in alignment – they not only understand the leader's vision, but they embrace it as their own personal quest.

This is the "west" we've been speaking of. This is what assures the group will continue their progress toward a common outcome, even if the leader is struck down.

So with the leader pointing the way and the herd on the move, the managers can then coach the team to accomplish the next steps in the process, whatever those might be, allowing the crew to handle the tasks involved in a way that works best for them.

I suspect many managers see their jobs as controlling the crew. This is understandable, but a fixation on retaining control is an open invitation to a management career of endless struggle and stress because nobody likes to be micro-managed.

The simple truth is that your operation is out of control! That may be an unnerving thought, but if you can make peace with the reality of that idea, your professional life will get significantly easier!

Unless you sit on somebody's shoulder and tell them what to do second-by-second all day (which isn't a great idea, even if it were possible), they will do what makes sense to them in the moment. In that regard, it's entirely out of your control.

Control is a myth. Don't fight it, just relax and accept it ... then focus your energies on keeping the herd moving roughly west!

42

16
Be in Alignment With Your Guests

Alignment within your organization is critical, of course ... but it's just as important that the organization be in alignment with the needs of your guests. After all, they're the ones you're in business to serve. If you're not doing things that are meaningful to them, they won't support you.

If your patrons are looking for a pleasant experience and you're only focused on how much money you can pry from their clutching fingers, the relationship won't endure.

However, if you're passionate about being a Place of Hospitality ... about making their day, every day ... the relationship will be effortless and mutually beneficial. They will patronize you more often (at full price!) and recommend you to their friends ... because they *want to.*

Alignment isn't at odds with profitability, but the money comes because others feel good about supporting you, not because you discounted your products or relentlessly pumped the sale of add-ons and extras.

Typical suggestive selling techniques may produce short term results, but unless it's done with enthusiasm and sincerity, it's not likely to make guests feel warm, fuzzy and anxious to return. If you get the sale tonight but lose the patron forever, that's the most costly sale you can make.

Do you have a larger purpose in alignment with what your market needs and wants?

Can you clearly put it into words?

Do you share it with your guests?

Does your staff know it and buy into it?

Does it drive every decision you make?

17
Chris the Dishwasher

A marginal performer may just be mis-assigned. This example may give you another way to look at performance:

When I was the foodservice director at the Olympic Training Center, I had a dishwasher, Chris, who just wasn't cutting it in the dish room. I liked him as a person, but there was a part of me that said if he couldn't make it in the dish room, he hadn't earned the right to go anywhere else. I could see termination looming in his future.

Chris had a job history like a lot of kids we see in the hospitality biz – three months in one job, six months in another – and it was looking like the OTC was going to be another repeat performance.

I reflected on what I should do about him and one day it hit me: Chris was never going to make it in the dish room because Chris didn't **want** to make it in the dish room.

Suddenly it all got simple. If I left him where he was, I would soon have to fire him. If I moved him to another position and it didn't work, he'd be gone as well.

But if I tried a different approach and it **did** work, everybody could win.

I took him aside one day and asked, "Chris, is it obvious to you where all this is headed?" Of course it was – he'd been in a similar situation in most every job he'd ever had.

My next move wasn't at all what he expected. I said, "It's obvious to me that this job isn't what you really want to be doing. What do you really want to do?" A bit stunned, he thought for a second and replied, "I want to go into the dining room."

Having nothing to lose, I agreed, with the understanding that it was either up or out – if things didn't work out in the dining room, he couldn't come back to the dish room. "You just watch me," he said.

The next opening that came up in the dining room went to Chris ... and he was doing pretty well. The exciting part, though, was what happened when we got into a project to upgrade the look of our salad bar.

The Salad Bar Breakthrough

A different staff member was responsible for setting up our salad bar every day. My specification on the salad bar was simple: I wanted to hear a spontaneous, positive reaction when the athletes first saw it. I wanted to hear an "Ooh" or a "Wow" or a "Doesn't that look good!" If it was your day to do the salad bar and you weren't hearing any comments, tweak it until you did.

I'd borrowed some garnishing videos from the Community College, put them up on the big screens in the afternoon and bought knives for all my dining room crew. They learned to make tomato roses and similar fancy touches, used them on the salad bar and we were hearing lots of good comments from the athletes.

Eventually it was Chris's turn to do the salad bar. From the time I walked in that morning, everyone was excited, "You've got to see Chris's salad bar," they all insisted, so I went to see what the buzz was about.

I immediately saw why they were excited. Chris had designed a beach scene with palm trees and surfers – everything made from fruit and vegetables – and none of which was on the videos!

When I asked him about it, he said, "Well, it seemed to me that if A was possible, then I could do B and if I could do B, I didn't see any reason why I couldn't do C!" Chris had caught on fire!

A Turning Point?

I don't know where Chris is today or what he's doing – he's probably not in foodservice any more – but I have to believe that event was a turning point for him. For perhaps the first time in his life, he discovered he could be good at something on his own terms! It just had to be a breakthrough experience for him!

Had I been obsessed with control, I probably would have handled Chris's poor performance by firing him.

If I had played it that way, the OTC would have lost a great worker and Chris would've had one more failure to confirm the idea that he was never going to amount to anything.

Had that happened, everyone would have lost.

By finding a way to help Chris continue to move west with the rest of us, a perfect, if somewhat counter-intuitive, solution appeared ... and everybody came out ahead!

As managers, I think we have a responsibility – both terrifying and incredibly exciting – to help our staff discover their excellence. I contend that every person is great at something, they may just not be great at the job we've put them in.

You've put a lot of time and money into orientation and training. Before you just cut somebody loose, throw that investment away and volunteer for the pain of finding and training another rookie, you might first see if there's another place in the organization that would be a better fit for their skills and interest.

You've got people in the dining room that should be in the kitchen, people in the kitchen that are naturals for maintenance, people in maintenance that want to be in the office ... and perhaps people in the office that ought to be in jail!

But make an honest effort to learn about the special skills and interests of each of your workers. When you understand them as people and not just cogs in the machine, you can make wiser decisions about where and how to use their unique talents ... or if the best career move for them is with another team.

Working in the best interests of your staff is always in the long-term best interests of the restaurant.

18
Your Real Job

As a manager, I believe your real job is not to *run* the joint, it's to teach your *staff* how to run the joint!

You'll never be able to move on to new projects (or get away for more personal time) unless your crew can assume some of the responsibilities that presently fall to you ... and the only way they'll be able to do that is if someone teaches them.

Disrespect
If you are doing anything that someone on your staff is capable of doing – and you're not giving it to them to do – that is disrespectful. You're standing in the way of their professional development. Stop it! Disrespect will quickly destroy relationships in any business.

Failure to delegate routine tasks may also deliver a message that you don't think the other person is capable of doing the job. Whether that particular conclusion is correct is irrelevant, your reluctance to delegate tasks, especially the simple ones, could be seen as your way of keeping power in your own hands.

The organization suffers because qualified people leave for jobs where they **can** advance their skills. At the same time, managers inadvertently perpetuate the overload that leads to exhaustion, stress and burnout.

Work Smarter
Take a look at where you're investing your time. For example, do you spend hours writing the schedule? There's no law that says you have to do it, only that a schedule needs to be done.

Once you have it down pat, teach someone on your staff to do it! At some point in your career someone trusted **you** with the job for the first time. Give your staff the same break. Delegation will be a relief to you and a job enhancement for them.

The same thinking applies to other typical tasks like taking inventory or doing most ordering. With a bit of coaching, someone on your staff can learn to handle these tasks as well (or better!) than you can ... and it'll be easy to monitor their progress and see how they're doing.

Start with Three Tasks

As a start, identify three activities that occupy your time – jobs that others on your staff may already be capable of doing. If these folks are willing to take on the new responsibilities, give the jobs to them.

Don't insist they do everything exactly the way you would. All you really need is consistency of the end result. If they can get the same or better results in less time without breaking any laws, why waste energy insisting on the manner in which that happens?

When you're comfortable the new tasks are being well-handled, identify three common jobs on your list that others on the staff are capable of *learning*. With your newly found free time, start teaching them what they need to know to assume those tasks as well.

The results of this process are simply wonderful! You take jobs that you've mastered and pass them along to people who are excited to get them! You get to continually reinvent your own job which keeps you fresh and excited while at the same time, your staff becomes more confident, more skilled and more invested in the success of your operation.

A few words of caution before you start, though:

There's a Difference Between Delegation and Abdication

As a world-class manager, you want to be sure your staff succeeds in their new work. Failure helps no one, so never turn anyone loose until they've been thoroughly coached or they may panic and fail.

Before you turn a job over to someone else, you may want to do it yourself until you've mastered it. In cases, where you know you just don't have the temperament for a particular task, delegating it to someone who does may work out better for everyone. It's OK if your staff knows more than you do.

48

Just a heads-up: if there are jobs that you have been constantly complaining to your staff about, delegating those could be seen as dumping. After all, if you hate them, why should anyone else be excited about taking them on?

Don't Delegate to Those Who Don't Want Responsibility

Not everyone wants to advance and it's futile to force a task onto someone who doesn't want it. That's dumping, not delegation. With a history of successful transitions, people will be comfortable that you're not setting them up to fail and will be more eager to tackle something new, particularly if you reward their achievement.

Reflect the New Responsibilities on the Pay Check

You must address the question of "what's in it for me?" It's only fair to reflect someone's increased contributions to your profitability on their paycheck. If you don't give for what you get, you'll find few volunteers for new duties.

Don't view delegation as increasing costs. Rather, see it as a means to bring more talent to bear on daily operations and break yourself free to identify ways to increase revenue. Even if delegation does nothing other than give you time to have a life(!), any additional costs will be more than offset by your own increase in productivity.

Expect Mistakes

A "mistake" only shows the extent of a person's understanding. We all slip a few times when taking on new challenges. Since no one likes to fail, making a big deal of an error will only destroy the desire to learn and add another "rule" to the book. (See Chapter 36)

Approach your job as a coach ("This is good, that's great, let's work on this part now.") and you'll do fine. Bear in mind that you are also learning – in this case, you're learning how to delegate successfully – and you should expect to make a mistake or two as you learn how to do it.

Does this mean that things will happen differently than the way you would have done them? Almost certainly. Does this mean you won't get the results you want? Not at all.

The right things will still happen – the herd will continue to move roughly west – but with fresh energy from many other people.

19
The Power of Presence

The secret to creating impact with others is presence.

Simply put, presence is a state of mind that is free from distraction. Your level of presence is the extent to which your mind is not occupied with thoughts unrelated to the project at hand.

Here are a few examples of what I mean:

Have you ever been talking to someone who was listening to you ... and then suddenly they **weren't** listening to you? They may even have been looking at you and nodding their heads as you spoke, but didn't you know when their attention was elsewhere?

Or have you been talking with someone on the phone who was doing something else at the same time? Even though you couldn't see them, wasn't it obvious you didn't have their full attention?

These are both instances of a distracted state of mind or what I'm calling a low level of presence.

Recall your experience of talking to someone who wasn't really listening to you. If you're like most people, you probably found their distracted behavior to be rude at best and infuriating at worst.

Distractions
A distracted state of mind creates irritation in other people. You know how incredibly annoying it can be to talk with someone whose mind has wandered. Yet we do the same thing to people constantly.

Somehow we've accepted the notion that the way to be efficient and get more done is to do several tasks at once. In fact, effectiveness comes from just the opposite approach.

Ever been on the telephone while working on the staff schedule and trying to handle a question from a crew member at the same time? Been there? Done that?

My guess is that neither the schedule, the person on the other end of the phone, or your staff member really got the attention they needed.

In all likelihood you probably had to go back to one or all of these folks for clarification, to correct mistakes or to make another try at resolving an issue that could easily have been handled if you were totally focused to begin with.

Lessons from Life

Imagine your two-year-old is looking for attention and you're busy. As they tug on your pant leg you say "Later, kid, I'm busy" without looking up from your work. Do they respond with, "Sure, Daddy, I understand"? Not a chance!

To take care of a two-year-old, drop what you're doing, get down eyeball to eyeball, give them your undivided attention for about five seconds and you'll buy yourself some time.

You may get a few minutes and you may get a few hours, but if kids don't get that degree of attention, they'll pull on you for the rest of their natural lives! Is that reasonably close?

It's no different if they're twenty-two. It's no different if they're sixty-two. Mainly, people want to know that you "got it" – that whatever they had to say actually got *through* to you. This can't happen if you're distracted.

The only difference between dealing with children and adults is that kids are more honest – they won't pretend they have your attention if they don't. Adults are more socially correct, but they're no less observant.

Presence and Productivity

The truth is that you can really only focus your attention on one thing at a time anyway. When you're talking with someone, there's nothing else you can be doing and no other place you can be at that moment. Be with people when you are with people.

Multi-tasking is a good way to screw up several things at once! None of the tasks gets your full attention, so none benefit from your best effort.

If you're preoccupied with extraneous thoughts, your attention is not fully with the person in front of you. Even if they don't call you on it, they'll spend the rest of the day trying to get your attention. As with children, you can deal with a situation in five seconds or five hours – the difference is just your level of presence when you do it.

The secret to productivity is to handle things exactly the way you would with a child. Drop distractions, be in the moment with the task, handle one item at a time and move on to the next project.

Presence (lack of distraction) will enable you to more accurately assess situations and quickly deal with them more effectively.

Presence and Service
In my service seminars, I point out that the reason guests leave a tip of 10% or 30% for doing essentially the same thing depends in large measure on the personal connection servers create with the guests. Presence increases the personal connection between people. In fact, without presence, there can be no personal connection at all.

I watched one server in a resort hotel increase his tips from 10-12% one night to 25-30% the next night by, as he said, "just trying to be AT the table when I'm at the table."

I had a manager say half his "people problems" disappeared when he started to BE with people when he was with them.

When your customers have a complaint or when your staff members have a question, what they want most is to feel that you really *hear* what they had to say. Most don't expect you to resolve their every concern on the spot, but they definitely want to sense that what they had to say was important to you.

Just as a distracted state of mind creates irritation in others, presence makes people feel more positive and better-served. You convey your caring by your level of presence and people highly value the message they get when you are in the moment with them.

In work with tipped employees (restaurant staff and hair stylists) we found increased presence improved their tips by as much as 250%!

If you've ever worked for someone who didn't listen, you know the feeling of being ignored. You can't tell someone who doesn't listen that they don't listen because ... well ... they don't listen!

People who don't listen think they do; they seldom have a clue that they're distracted. Your challenge is to be sure you aren't guilty of the same sin when someone needs your attention.

Presence and Enjoyment

There's a direct connection between your level of presence and the enjoyment you derive from what you're doing. Have you ever been so immersed in an activity that you totally lost track of time? If so, you've had the experience of operating in a state of high presence. You were in the moment without distracting thoughts.

If you find your job irritating, the only problem may be that you're distracted. Quiet your mind, drop distractions, slow down to the speed of life, and see how enjoyable things will suddenly become. Anything worth doing is worth doing with your full participation.

A Natural State

Presence isn't something unnatural – it's something we're all born with. Little babies have amazing presence because their heads aren't yet all cluttered up with thoughts – they only know how to deal with what's right in front of them at the moment.

This sounds too simple, but look what happens when you bring a newborn baby into a room. Everyone's attention shifts to the baby. People feel better, start to smile and forget their own problems for a few minutes. The baby isn't *doing* anything – it's just being there – yet everyone around them feels more positive.

We call it the Helium Principle: If you maintain a positive state of mind, other people will naturally rise to that.

This demonstrates the power of presence to make others feel more positive.

High presence is our birthright, but it's also something we can easily lose sight of as the pace of business speeds up, our lives become increasingly complex and we take on more responsibilities.

Start to Notice

It's unrealistic to think you will always operate without distractions, but you **can** start to become aware of distracting thoughts when they start to clutter your mind.

One way to tell this is happening is when the people you're talking with get restless or when you see a glazed look in their eyes. If your attention wanders off track, so will theirs.

The good news is that simply becoming aware of the fact that you're distracted will automatically start you self-correcting again. When you notice that you're drifting off track, gently let go of stray thoughts and allow your attention return to the task at hand.

Your increased presence will make whoever you are with feel better-served and bring more impact to your message.

20
Motivation

Do you think the manager's job is to motivate the staff? If so, you're making your job more difficult.

When most people talk about motivation, they're usually referring to external motivation. If it's your job to motivate someone, then it must be coming from the outside, right?

There are basically two ways you can provide external motivation: one is the carrot and the stick, the other is the gun to the back of the head!

There's no doubt you can make things happen using these two models ... but for either approach to be effective over time, you'll keep needing bigger and bigger carrots ... and you'll need bigger guns as well!

The other problem is that if this is the only way you can achieve results in your organization, if you're not there holding the stick (or the gun), nothing happens. If you're regularly working 70+ hours a week, it may be because you've inadvertently set things up this way.

At the heart of the classic view of motivation are two simple ideas: Rewarding an activity will get you more of it. Punishing an activity will get you less of it.

That model holds until rewards and punishments meet the growing awareness that people are increasingly motivated by their own internal factors more than they are by the external ones.

Money, the most powerful reward, is important, of course, but lack of money is a more powerful force than an abundance of it. Pay someone less than they feel is right and their focus will be on the unfairness of their situation and the anxiety of their circumstances.

The best use of money as a motivator is to pay people enough to take the issue of money off the table.

Think about it: absent any money worries, how much more energy would your staff bring to the job? For that matter, how much would your peace of mind improve if you had no concerns about meeting your financial commitments?

Once compensation meets needs, rewards and punishments can have exactly the opposite effect you intend. The practices designed to increase motivation dampen it. Tactics aimed at boosting creativity can reduce it. Programs intended to promote good deeds can make them disappear.

Instead of restraining negative behavior, rewards and punishments can actually give rise to cheating, addiction and dangerously limited thinking. This doesn't hold true in all cases, of course, but research demonstrates many common practices whose effectiveness we take for granted can actually give us less of what we want and more of what we don't want.

Mark Twain wrote, "Work consists of whatever a body is **obliged** to do. Play consists of whatever a body is not obliged to do."

He went on to write, "There are wealthy gentlemen in England who drive four-horse passenger coaches twenty or thirty miles on a daily line in the summer. The privilege costs them considerable money, but if they were offered wages for the service, that would turn it into work and then they would resign."

We've been taught that people do what they are rewarded for. We've built a management model around incentives and bonuses, but the reward itself can turn an interesting task into a struggle; turn play into work.

By diminishing internal motivation, rewards can actually destroy performance, creativity and behavior.

Behavioral research shows that rewards themselves are not a disincentive. The problem arises when those rewards are contingent and expected – if you do this, then you'll get that.

Receiving an unexpected reward didn't impact internal motivation, so why would an expected reward have the opposite effect?

It seems that "If-Then" rewards require people to give up some of their autonomy. Like the gentlemen driving carriages for money instead of fun, they are no longer fully controlling their lives ... and that can drain an activity of its enjoyment.

My late colleague, human relations consultant Robert Kausen made these observations:

> "People naturally want to produce excellent results. Contrary to the popular misconception, employees really do want to work, and they instinctively want to produce top notch results. When we excel, we feel wonderful. When we throw ourselves into our work, we experience a natural high that inspires us to do even better.
>
> High performance feels wonderful and holding back is no fun. It is the total involvement, not the activity, that results in the enjoyment. The enemy of involvement is distraction. You cannot quiet someone else's distracted mind, but you can provide a sane climate that promotes healthy mental functioning, thus greater involvement and impact."

Does that sound like a little more workable model of motivation and behavior? Let's look at the dynamics of that more closely.

21
Climate

Did you ever go to another couple's house and they'd had a major argument just before you arrived? Couldn't you tell? Not from anything they said or anything you could see, but couldn't you *feel* the negative vibes in the air?

Or when you go into a competitor's restaurant, can't you immediately tell when the kitchen and the dining room are having a feud or when the manager has just publicly chewed out a waiter? Again, you can feel it ... and it feels uncomfortable.

On the other hand, when you're in the presence of two people who are very much in love – perhaps at a wedding – doesn't that feeling pervade the room and make everyone feel more warm and fuzzy?

What you're feeling is the climate – the feeling on the job. Think of climate as the level of mental health in the organization; the collective states of mind of everyone on the team.

The good news and the bad news is that the climate of a company always starts at the top. In other words, your organization will always tend to reflect your own thinking. When you're calm and focused, the whole place is calm and focused; when you panic, everyone panics.

There's a relationship between climate and motivation – or any behavior, for that matter – and if you can understand how they interrelate, it will make a major difference in your ability to influence results.

We talk about the idea of above the line and below the line behavior but understand there really isn't a line. Above the line is productive functioning, below the line is dysfunctional. We could also have called it good mood/bad mood, secure/insecure or hospitable/inhospitable.

It's only a model but hopefully the figure on the next page it will help you start to understand the dynamics and the relationship between thinking and behavior.

The chart below shows the relationship between the climate in the organization, the feeling on the job and what you tend to see for behavior at various levels.

ORGANIZATIONAL BEHAVIOR

CLIMATE	FEELING ON THE JOB	ORGANIZATIONAL BEHAVIOR	
EXHILARATION	*Effortless*	Intuitive	Creativity
		Magic	Self-Management
		Synergy	Customer Delight
INSPIRATION	*Alive*	Teamwork	Productivity
		Initiative	Motivation
		Clarity	Professional Curiosity
CONTENTMENT	*Hopeful*	Flexibility	Confidence
		Cooperation	Humorous
		Extra Effort	Attention to Detail
TENSION	*Stressed*	Gossip	Whining & Complaining
		Tardiness	Defensiveness
		Distrust	Resistance to Change
UNHAPPINESS	*Upset*	Suspicion	No-Shows
		Accidents	Cliques
		Turnover	Disagreements
CHAOS	*Frightening*	Fights	Theft
		Subversion	Arguments
		Anger	Walk-Outs

Below the Line Behavior

In a very low climate – call it chaos – the feeling on the job is simply frightening. The behaviors you tend to see at that level are fights, theft, anger and walkouts. If you've ever worked in an organization that was running in chaos, you know that it can be terrifying! "Get me out of here!"

As it gets a little bit better, maybe you reach a point of unhappiness. The feeling on the job is upset and the behavior is very defensive. People form cliques. Accidents and minor lapses of attention increase.

In larger companies, people hoard information and build empires. Staff turnover is high because people don't want to hang out in such an environment. It's better than chaos, but it is still dysfunctional behavior.

Many businesses, particularly restaurants, run in tension. The feeling on the job is stressed and the behavior you likely see is gossip, whining, distrust, complaining and petty sniping. Again, organizational functioning has improved a bit, but you're still below the line and comparatively unproductive.

Above the Line Behavior

As you get above the line, you start to get into more productive thinking. Contentment and hope return. You start to see spontaneous, positive humor (as opposed to negative joke-at-someone's-expense kind of humor.) The organization lightens up.

As it gets even better, you reach a level we might call inspiration. The feeling in the company is alive. You will see teamwork, natural internal motivation and high productivity.

In a very high climate – call it exhilaration – there's a feeling of effortlessness on the job. You'll see creativity, magic, and a staff who manages themselves.

The level of customer service is high because the feeling is rather like being in love. You don't have to talk to somebody in love about taking care of people – people in love take care of people cause they just want to take care of people.

In a positive climate you naturally get teamwork, caring and motivation; in a negative climate, good luck! A positive climate will produce a high performance organization by default; in a negative climate, every task is a struggle.

The key to understanding organizational behavior lies in grasping two important principles:

Behavior is a very predictable symptom of the climate.

To change work performance, change the work environment.

22
The Day from Hell

The notion that behavior in the organization is simply a reflection of the climate is so simple and yet revolutionary when we compare it to the way we always thought things worked. Because I know this idea can seem too simple to be applicable in the real world, let me share a personal example to show the power of this understanding:

Back in another life, I was hired by the U.S. Olympic Committee to take over the foodservice at the Olympic Training Center (OTC) in Colorado Springs. The OTC is a year-round operation whose dining program at the time was in desperate need of a major overhaul. In fact, foodservice had consistently been the #1 source of complaints from athletes in training.

How Low Can You Go?

To underscore how bad things were, the day I arrived to take over the dining operations we had two knife fights in the kitchen!

Apparently, two of my workers got into an argument and were waving kitchen knives at each other with some degree of seriousness.

No damage was done (and neither had packed their own knife in!) but everyone was nervous for a few minutes. This had all the signs of being a real "Day from Hell!"

I had received some excellent training in my professional career, but knife fights weren't something we had ever talked much about!

I hope you never encounter a predicament like this in your own operation but it makes for an interesting case study. So just for a moment, imagine yourself in my position. Take a deep breath and think about how you might have approached the situation.

The Classic Approach

In the old "management expertise" (cop-based) mode that I spent so many years refining, my first response to this predicament would likely have been to fire – or at least suspend or put on probation – the people involved. You've got to deliver a clear message that this is unacceptable behavior, right?

After that, if I didn't already have one, I would have written a clear policy about knife fights. It would have specified that engaging in such dangerous behavior was unacceptable conduct and could be considered grounds for immediate dismissal. I'd have everyone sign it and put it in their personnel files.

Finally, I would have held a special staff meeting to explain the policy. I would have made sure my staff understood how behavior of this sort worked against everything we were trying to accomplish. I would have talked about the importance of teamwork and cooperation, probably with some Olympic analogies.

I would have shared my vision for the operation and tried to get my crew excited about what we could do together. It would have been an inspirational session designed to help my staff see that we were all in this together and we had to work together to succeed in providing memorable service to the athletes.

What's Wrong with this Picture?

I share this story in many of my management seminars. When we reach this point in the discussion, the majority of group generally agrees that they'd probably take an approach similar to the one I just described.

My next question to them (and to you) is this:

> *"How effective do you think this strategy would be at eliminating knife fights forever and always in your operation?"*

Somewhat sheepishly, they confess that while there might be some short term effect, they don't really expect that much would change over the long haul.

The conversation usually goes like this:

"Is this more or less what you would do?"
"Well ... yes."
"Would it work?"
"Well ... no."
"But it's still the way you'd handle it?"
"Well ... yes."

Do you see the problem?

Had I followed this scenario when the knife fight happened, this strategy wouldn't have worked either. Worse yet, when I didn't get the results I wanted, I would have looked at how to write a better memo or gone to a seminar on how to hold more effective staff meetings!

I'd worry that perhaps I didn't come down on them fast enough and hard enough. It would never have occurred to me that approaching the problem in this manner was a futile exercise from the outset. This is what I mean about becoming better and better at doing things that don't work!

Applying a New Understanding
When the knife fights came up, however, I had arrived at a different understanding about the real cause of behavior. I had started to recognize that behavior was just a symptom of a person's level of thinking as reflected in the climate of the organization.

Instead of seeing the knife fight as a statement about the people involved, I saw it as the indication of a low climate. The offenders in the incident were simply in a state of mind where swinging knives at each other seemed like an appropriate way to settle a dispute.

I understood that the only way the behavior would change was when the level of thinking that created it changed.

I talked with the two combatants and suggested that carving up their co-workers wasn't a particularly cool thing to do, but I never addressed the behavior directly. My conversation went more like this:

"Given what happened, it's obvious that something has you really frustrated. What's wrong with this chicken outfit? What's making your job tough and what do you think we can do about it?"

My goal was to **listen** – not for hard facts, but for an insight into what was weighing heavily on their minds. Whatever their pre-occupation, it was making their lives (and mine!) more difficult, affecting their thinking and leading to unproductive behavior.

To accomplish this goal, I just had to listen without judgement – be "dumb as dirt" if you will. I had come to realize that the simple act of nonjudgmental listening was a major aid in helping people return to a healthier state of mind.

I knew the behavior would change when their level of personal security and well-being increased. In a higher state of mind, the notion of attacking someone else would never even occur to them. The behavior wasn't the problem, it was actually just a symptom.

Learn from Your Staff
My discussions were revealing. I quickly discovered we had many more people on staff than we needed.

Activity at the OTC was very seasonal at that point – very busy in the summer, very slow in the winter. I took over in November to find all the summer workers were still on the payroll.

Apparently my predecessor had figured he'd let the new guy fire them, so he just cut everyone's hours back. People didn't have enough hours to pay their bills, but they couldn't afford to quit their jobs. I would have been frustrated in that situation, too!

This Is Not Management by Meditation
It became obvious that to eliminate the frustration I'd first have to deal with the lack of hours. I held a series of one-on-one interviews to get a feel for my new staff as individuals and get a sense of where their heads were. Then I resolved the issue the only way I could – I fired half of them!

My termination list included those I believed were the most negative or angry (in the lowest states of mind) but on a different day it might well have been a different group. Even if **everyone** had been in a great mood, I **still** would have let half of them go!

"OK, everyone has full hours, so that's not an issue. What's the next thing we have to work on?" (As an interesting side note, the knife-fighters were among the people I kept on the team!)

"Black Wednesday," the day I trimmed the staff, was nobody's idea of a good time ... but when it was over, it was over and everyone immediately felt better. The whiners and complainers were gone and everyone who remained had a full schedule.

With the issue of adequate hours eliminated, the general work climate improved. In a more positive state of mind, people started to suggest other areas that could be corrected. When we uncovered an irritant, we fixed it ... and every time we eliminated a distraction, the climate became more positive.

Some Interesting Things Happened
The next day, not only had knife fights stopped, but the idea would never enter anyone's mind! In fact, we never talked about knife fights again and never had a similar incident.

Some other interesting things happened: Within two months we had become the #1 source of compliments from the athletes and coaches – all the more remarkable because it was done with the same workers who had once made us the #1 source of complaints!

We didn't have sales as such, but within six months, the number of times athletes came in had gone from 1.3 times a day to 2.5 times a day. Labor cost per meal dropped more than 20 percent and our food cost per meal declined nearly 25 percent on the same menu. Staff turnover went from 300% to 25% with no change in wages!

4½ years later when I left the OTC, the people involved in the knife fights were still on staff and were among our most productive workers ... and most managers would have thrown them away!

Behavior Is Only a Symptom
I share this story to illustrate the simple power that comes from understanding how the climate in a company determines the behavior on the job.

At the time the knife fight issue came up, I couldn't have told you for sure if handling things this way would succeed ... but I was certain that "kicking butt and taking names" would fail.

Anything you do that contributes to goodwill and trust will bring the level up and you'll get those behaviors that come from a positive climate.

Anything you do that contributes to fear and insecurity will bring the level down.

It's important not to think of this story as a lesson on how to handle knife fights but just as an anecdote about how one person applied the principles of climate and behavior to a real business problem.

The power doesn't reside in any sort of technique but rather in the understanding. I promise if you truly understand the principles at work, you will instinctively know what to do in most any situation. Not only that, but your approach is likely to work every time!

There are several management qualities that can improve the climate and lead to self-motivation in the organization. In the next few chapters we'll look at a few of them.

23
Listening

One of the best things you can do to improve the climate is to listen. Listen with curiosity, listen with humility, listen for an insight.

(Most people don't listen, they just wait their turn to talk ... some don't even wait!)

Phillips Mentor Program
Probably the best example of a structured listening program came out of a management retreat that I facilitated for Phillips Seafood Restaurants, a group of high volume operations in the Chesapeake Bay area.

It was in the late 90s and the meeting's theme was "Phillips in the Year 2000" – what does the company look like in the next century? Not many organizations would take the time to look at that.

Somebody said, "Phillips in the year 2000 is a people company." I responded, "Well, that sounds good ... but what does a people company *look* like? If this were a people company, how could we tell it from an organization that *wasn't* a people company?"

We kicked this around in the group and what came out of that was what they called a mentor program.

Everyone on the hourly staff was assigned a manager (not their regular supervisor) to be their mentor – rather like a big brother or sister. Phillips is a big organization and every manager ended up with about 30 people reporting to them as part of this program.

Under the mentor program they designed, the staff was guaranteed 30 minutes a month of uninterrupted one-on-one time with their mentor to talk about whatever *they* wanted to talk about. It wasn't a training session or a sermon from the mount. They already had ways to do that.

You can do the math on this ... and many of the managers were starting to have a little trouble with the idea as well.

Thirty people at half an hour apiece is fifteen hours a month, the managers were thinking. "Where am I going to find fifteen hours a month? I don't have enough time to do my job as it is."

Mark Sneed, then their Operations VP, put it in perspective when he said, "If this is what we say we are as a company today, this *is* what we are as a company. You have an option of whether you want to stay with the company or not, but if this is what we agree to do, you don't have an option of whether you're going to participate in this program."

I talked to Mark about six months later to find out how it was going. He said the first couple of months were a bit shaky as everyone learned the routine. However, he said that if he tried to eliminate it now, he'd probably lose all of his managers and most of his staff!

"Without question, it's the best single thing we ever did," he said. "We got all the things we expected. Productivity is up, turnover is down, we rather expected that."

"What we got that we didn't expect is that our level of customer service has measurably improved. Perhaps because our staff has a model of one-on-one interaction with their managers, they deal with the guests one-on-one as well."

I asked him about the time requirements the managers had been so concerned about. He said that was the easiest part of it. The managers had come to realize the reason they never had enough time was because they'd spent most of their day putting out fires.

"We just don't have those fires anymore," he said. "If Michael graduates in June, we know in February what Michael is going to do because we're talking to him all the time. Best of all, the working environment in the restaurants has improved immensely."

I'll talk more about listening in Chapter 52.

24
The Benefit of the Doubt

Maybe this is just another way to listen, but maintain a benefit-of-the-doubt stance with your staff. Understand that there is always more information than you have and it's respectful to assume the best until you have all the facts.

If Karen has been late three times and is late again, it's easy to jump to a conclusion about Karen. But maybe this is the day her child got hit by a car and she's had more important things on her mind. You don't know the details, but you can be sure that Karen would not have been late unless Karen had a reason that made sense to *her*!

The fact that her reasoning may or may not make sense to you is not required. You want to find out what her thinking was before you make up her mind. It doesn't mean you'll buy her story, but you want to hear it before you decide how to proceed.

What You Think Is What You Get
It's interesting that when you assume the best, you tend to get it. I know when I saw my staff as a bunch of crooks who'd rob me blind if I didn't watch them every minute, I wasn't disappointed.

And when I saw them as intelligent adults who were doing the best they could and wanted to make a contribution if they just had an opportunity to do that, I wasn't disappointed either.

In some cases, it was the same people. *They* didn't change ... *I* did.

25
Serve Your Staff

The analogy that comes to mind is the sport of curling. It's rather like shuffleboard on ice. One member of the team gives a heavy stone a push down the ice toward a target while two other team members move along ahead of the stone, sweeping the ice with brooms.

The sweepers have two jobs: first, to get everything out of the way of the stone that might impede its progress and make sure the stone has a totally clean sheet of ice to run on.

Second, depending on whether they sweep faster or slower, they make the ice a little faster or slower and that determines how far the stone will go and how it will behave (curl). But momentum and direction are already established by somebody else.

Like the stone, your organization has a momentum – it is moving in a direction (roughly west, we hope!) I'd rather be up in front with the broom keeping the ice clear, than to be in the back, trying to force the stone through the debris.

In the middle of the rush, the best place I can be is at the restaurant supply store getting the ladles the kitchen needs to get through the meal, not yelling at them about producing the menu. They know how to do that. What they need are the tools to do it!

When the rush is over, we can look at how we ran out of ladles and how we can keep that from happening again, but in the heat of battle, my job is to make sure they have all the tools they need to do their jobs and they know how to use them.

The manager's traditional job has been to push the company through any obstacles that lie in its path. This new model recognizes that organizations and workers have their own momentum.

The proper focus of management should be to keep that energy flowing unimpeded rather than trying to force the movement.

26
Value and Respect Your Staff

On one level, think of what it would be like if everybody walked out on you in the middle of the rush. But on an entirely different level, when you allow yourself to connect with the staff as human beings, you will be moved by their innocence and heroism.

Everyday Heroism
I think it's heroic to be a single mother raising three children alone. I think it's heroic to be sixteen – it's a lot harder now than it was when we did it! When you establish this human connection, you naturally start treating people well because you'll understand they deserve the best care you can muster.

You have people on your staff who are facing huge challenges. They have family problems, financial issues and many other struggles in their lives, but they show up every day and do the best they can.

When you let yourself be touched by the warm feeling of deep respect for someone as a human being, you will start to take better care of your crew because you'll just see that they're worth the extra effort.

When you deal with your staff this way, they'll tend to deal with your guests this way ... and you'll all get to enjoy a more productive, positive working environment.

27
Value a Free and Clear Mind

The most potent thing you bring to the job is your own mental health. Remember that the climate of the organization always starts at the top. The reason you can't regularly work 70+ hours a week is that your mind gets scrambled, your own level of well-being drops and the productivity of the entire organization suffers.

This is part of a radical concept called "Have a Life!"

If hard work made money, you'd be among the richest people on the planet! You got where you are based on what you could **do**, but your future success will be based on what you can **get done**.

Anything you are doing right now, someone on your staff is capable of doing or eventually learning how to do ... but the only thing you can't give away is the vision – your sense of what your company could be. Vision is clarity about what "west" looks like for your organization and that vision only comes from a quiet mind.

So you must be sure to give yourself some quiet time. If that's playing with the kids, do it. If puttering in the garden, fly fishing or playing golf quiets your mind down, at this stage of your career it is an appropriate business activity ... and you can tell your boss I said so!

Clearing Your Mind
I have a good friend and client in Nags Head, North Carolina. He loved to play golf but he never played as often as he wanted because his restaurant was crazy busy and felt guilty about being gone.

The first time I worked with his managers I asked them what it was like when he finally took some time off to play golf. They sighed, "Oh, it's **so** nice!"

"By the time he realizes he's got to get out of here, he is such a pain in the butt. When he leaves, we can actually get some work done.

And when he comes back he's in such a great mood. He's got all these marvelous ideas, and he's so appreciative of us. It's just fantastic!"

So while he's thinking he can't leave, his staff is thinking, "Why won't he get out of here?"

As a footnote, I'm happy to report that he finally caught on. He plays golf regularly now and funny thing: the lower his handicap gets, the better his restaurant seems to run!

This is the power of the quiet mind ... and it doesn't matter if you're meditating, playing with the kids or reading a book. The value and the vision comes from slowing down and allowing your mind to clear.

Leaders respect the need to regularly get away from day-to-day tasks, and open themselves to fresh insights. As a recovering workaholic, I know the Puritan ethic that runs deep in our culture can make you feel guilty for "goofing off," but giving yourself quiet time is hardly dogging it. In the long run it's probably the most productive time you can spend.

I believe that leaders have an obligation to regularly get away from daily tasks and allow time for reflection. This may well be your most important business activity.

Only from a free and clear mind are you likely to dream the dreams that will establish the future direction of your operation.

28
Support Your Staff

In the long run, the only way your company can succeed is if your staff succeeds. This sounds obvious, but somewhere we got the idea that we could prosper over the bodies of our crew.

Perhaps that came from the days when it seemed like we had disposable labor; when we could treat people any way we wanted because we had a line of people waiting to take their jobs if they burned out and quit.

(You may have noticed the labor market isn't like that anymore!)

When you select people to become part of your staff, it should represent a commitment on the part of the company – supported by your words and deeds – to encourage and support their personal and professional development.

If you're uncomfortable about making that level of commitment to an individual staffer, perhaps you shouldn't bring that person on board.

29
Respect the Power of the Climate

A compassionate leader understands that staff members are always doing exactly what makes sense to them in the moment given their conditioned thinking and their state of mind.

No matter what you may be tempted to think, negative attitudes and substandard performance are usually just innocent conduct, not some sort of willful treachery.

Management becomes an easier, more enjoyable game to play when you respect the power of climate. Instead of cluttering your head with new techniques, all you need to do is understand what affects the climate and use that to guide your actions.

Implement more of those things that foster goodwill and trust and eliminate any practices that contribute to fear and insecurity. I guarantee the climate will improve measurably.

Almost everything you want to happen in your company will seem to happen practically on its own in a positive work climate. Hospitality will happen. Caring will happen. Teamwork will happen. Productivity will happen. Creativity and exceptional service will happen. Morale will improve, accidents will decline and the campers will be much happier.

If that sounds too easy, then you're on the right track.

Organizations Have Moods, Too
When I'd hear whining and complaining at the OTC (and it would happen), it would just be a wake-up call that I'd been spending too much time in the office. So I'd make it a point to walk around, talk with my crew and find out what they needed.

I'd swap stories with the cooks, notice things that were going well and make a point to compliment them on their progress. The climate would improve and all that negative behavior would just disappear.

In a more positive climate, many of the problems you spend your time dealing with now probably won't even show up. (Well, perhaps they will, but in a higher climate, a problem just looks like one more thing to handle and people hardly notice.)

30
Set a Personal Example

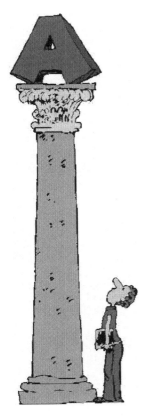

The suggestion you probably didn't want to hear is that you must set a personal example. You can't kick butt, take names and then say "Go love the guests." It's not going to work.

You are the role model whether you want the job or not.

If you want your staff to show up on time, show up on time. Want them to dress well? Dress well. Do you want them to listen? Listen. Do you want them to be open to new ideas? Be open to new ideas.

It also helps to realize that the way *you* treat your staff is the way *they* will treat your guests. When you lose it, the whole place loses it. When you're stressed out, the whole place stresses out.

When the atmosphere in your business is calm and your staff is attentive and relaxed, your patrons will be inclined to return more often.

That warm fuzzy feeling also improves the climate and makes the company a more attractive place to work. What's not to like about that?

31
What's Your Problem?

I know, you don't have problems, you only have challenges. You might say they're not problems, they're opportunities.

I acknowledge it's less paralyzing to think of your issues as opportunities rather than problems, but whatever euphemisms you use, you're still left with a problem in drag! Do you think that adopting different wording ever really changes things for most people?

However, problems (challenges, opportunities or whatever) are a daily fact of life and dealing with them seems to define the job of most managers. So let's take another look at problems, not from a semantic point of view but with an eye toward reaching a different understanding of what is and what is not really a problem.

Problems

As a start, a problem is merely a situation you don't yet have a handle on. Think about that for a minute.

The only reason you would see a situation as a problem is that you just can't quite figure out how to deal with it at the moment. Certainly if you knew how to handle it, it wouldn't be much of a problem. A nuisance, perhaps, but not really a problem.

If you're honest with yourself, you must admit that virtually every situation you face in life, personal or professional, ultimately has a workable solution. So instead of a major dilemma, all you're really facing is an event where the answer isn't yet apparent to you.

You know there's a solution, you just have to figure out how and where to find it. So there's really no problem.

Conditions

Any situation where there truly is no possible resolution isn't a problem, it's a condition.

For example, gravity is a condition. You can love gravity or you can hate it but there's nothing you can do to change it! Because gravity is a condition, you'd be wise to simply accept it and devote your energies to more productive pursuits than complaining about it.

What other "problems" do you face every day (and waste time getting upset about) that are, in fact, really conditions? Government regulations? Seasonality? Taxes? Aging?

Telling the Difference

You may still wonder how you can tell what's a condition and what is, in fact, a problem. If making the distinction is elusive, you're going to love Chapter 38!

32
Problem Solving

Do you define your job as being a problem-solver? Countless managers who follow the cop model do. "Find things that are wrong and fix them" is the order of the day for many, perhaps even most, managers.

The sentiment is admirable but have you noticed what you get when you define yourself as a problem-solver? That's right – more problems!

In fact, when you define yourself as a problem-solver, you **need** to have problems in order to justify your existence. It's the way you can feel that you're earning your keep. You may even look for situations to fix (they're never hard to find.) Worse yet, you may actually encourage people to bring you their problems so you can "do your job."

Solving problems is better than not solving problems, but every time you take on someone else's problem, it actually causes the operation to move backwards ... or at least prevents it from moving forward as quickly.

Let me explain what I mean:

Gaining Experience
The odds are you already have skill in resolving a wide range of operating issues. You may even pride yourself on your depth of experience ... and you should.

But when you assume the role of problem-solver, you're not likely to learn anything you didn't already know. After all, you've already learned how to solve the problem. Handling repetitive issues isn't likely to be a learning experience for you, merely a chance to make yourself feel useful.

The bigger danger when you take on the role of problem-solver is that you deprive your staff of an opportunity to learn for themselves what you learned by trial and error over the years. In fact, when you take on the responsibility to fix things, you're actually standing in the way of their professional development. Stop it!

Anything you are doing right now is a task they'll eventually have to learn in order to advance. When you grab the reins, the only thing your staff gets trained to do is to bring their problems to you.

The next time a similar problem arises, you'll get another task laid at your feet ... and they'll take a cigarette break!

If this is your idea of a good time, have at it, but I suggest the practice is detrimental to the well-being of your organization ... and hazardous to your own mental health as well.

Have a Life!
The complaint I most often hear voiced by managers is that the hours are too long and they don't have a life.

If you feel you don't have a life because you're working endless hours in a perpetual problem-solving mode, who do you think the culprit is? The trouble lies not with the business itself, but in your own belief that your job is to solve problems!

Let me take some pressure off and suggest that the manager's real job is not to *solve* the problems but to *find* the solutions; not to *have* the answers, but to be able to *find* the answers.

Note that there's nothing in these definitions that requires the manager to be the one to wrestle with every problem that arises.

Barring the occasional major disaster, your job as a manager is to help the staff learn how to deal with their own issues ... and that requires that you decline to take on any problem that could (or should) more properly be handled by someone else in the organization.

33
Finding Solutions

If Not the Manager, Who?

To determine who should have the responsibility for finding an answer to any given operating problem, ask yourself two questions:

Whose behavior has to change in order for this issue to be resolved?

Whose performance is most affected by the fact that this problem exists?

The answers to these two questions will point you directly to the person or persons who should tackle the problem.

If you'll permit me another example to illustrate this point, perhaps it will help you grasp what I'm getting at. Even if you don't offer bar service, I'm sure you can find parallels in your own workplace.

Where's My Drink?

Let's say you're getting complaints that it's taking a long time for drinks to arrive at the table. Whose problem is it?

In the typical management model, the manager sees it as her problem to solve. If she takes the problem on, she'll have to make sure she really knows the intimate realities of what everyone's job is like – an extremely difficult task.

Then she must formulate a realistic approach to solve the problem, get all the members of the staff to buy in (or force it down their throats), then follow up to make sure everyone does what they're "supposed" to do to implement the solution.

It's a lot of thankless work and it's likely tie her up for days or even weeks. Worse yet, there's still no guarantee that she'll truly have a long-term solution to the problem.

Plan B

Let's work on the slow drink issue with the idea that the manager's job is only to be able to *find* the answer. In this scenario, the first question is whose behavior has to change?

It could be the bartender ... or there could be a glitch in the way drinks are ordered or delivered, making servers likely parties.

Next, whose performance is most affected? It may be the bartender, the cocktail servers or the dining room servers.

By answering those two simple questions, you've just identified a group of people who are not only invested in finding an answer to the slow drinks question, but who can actually implement a solution once they agree on what it is ... and none of them is the manager!

It's their problem to solve. Put them in a room, turn them loose and see what they come up with. You may be surprised at the wisdom and insight they will bring to the table once they've been trusted to find their own answers.

Oh, and implementation will be quick and easy. People don't argue with their own information and since they came up with the solution, they will do whatever is necessary to make it work!

Everybody wins!

34
Give Your Job Away

All the great pilot training in the world will never make anyone a great pilot. At some point they have to solo!

If you never give your staff the chance to solo – the opportunity to work without a net and test their own ideas without a manager second-guessing and pre-approving every move – they'll never find out how good they are. They will continue to bring every little decision to you for action or approval before they make a move.

Putting the responsibility back on your team to find their own answers may slow things down a bit in the beginning, but it took you awhile (and probably a few spectacular failures) to develop the skills you have today. Don't deprive your staff of the opportunity to make their own mistakes.

Besides, they couldn't mess it up any worse than **you** did when you were first learning, could they?

I'm not suggesting the inmates should run the asylum. The job of the management is still to assure the company is proceeding smoothly in the right direction, but this isn't the same as the manager doing all of it herself.

In fact, the less essential management is to resolving the issues of the day, and the more problem-solving is encouraged and supported at the staff level, the smoother the operation will run and the happier the staff will be!

35
Taking Ownership

You hear a lot of horror stories about airlines these days. As a frequent flyer, I don't think the problem is that airlines don't know how to get it right. I think the problem is that they just aren't doing it.

I suspect if it were left to the workers rather than the "suits" to call the shots necessary to get the results, things would run a lot smoother. Unfortunately, it usually seems that "management" – particularly absentee management – often makes things harder rather than easier.

One of the first things I learned as a young naval officer is that the Chiefs (senior NCOs) really run the Navy. I discovered that the most effective thing I could do was to establish some direction for my unit, get buy-in from the crew and run interference so they could do what they knew needed to be done to get us there.

All of which brings me to my point. I hear a lot of managers talk about wanting their staff to take ownership of their performance. That's fine as far as it goes, but **there can be no ownership without something to own!**

In order for your staff to "own" something in the sense we're speaking of here, they must have the latitude to do it their way without the need for prior approval. They must feel free to achieve the desired results in a way that makes sense to *them* in the moment and be willing to be held responsible for the results they achieve.

Nobody will take ownership if the requirement is that they do it the way you would have done it nor will it happen if they need approval from a manager or supervisor at each step along the way before they can act. For better or worse, it must be *their* call and *their* reputation on the line.

Does it scare you to think of giving your crew this kind of latitude? Certainly you don't turn anyone loose until they have been thoroughly coached, but you'll be amazed at how your staff will excel once you get your own ego out of the way.

Still think it can never work? Nordstrom's [department store] built a reputation for legendary service with this very notion. Their "staff manual" is a card. On one side is the Nordstrom logo. On the other it simply says, "Use your own best judgment under all circumstances. There will be no other rules. If you have questions on how to interpret this, see your supervisor."

If you want people to take ownership, you must let them own something where they alone determine the plan of attack and where they alone are accountable for the results. Try it. They'll like it!

Back at the Olympics
Here's another example from the OTC to illustrate the point:

Within a week after my arrival at the OTC, my staff was doing almost everything my predecessor had taken on as his job.

For example, he would come in at 5:00am to do the ordering. I looked at that and thought, a) I don't know how to order for this operation, b) I don't want to do the ordering and, c) I'm not the best person to do the ordering even if I knew how and wanted to do it!

I asked my chef if he'd like to handle it ... and I thought he was going to hug me! He said, "I spend half my day cleaning up the messes that [the old manager] makes because he doesn't know what I have and he doesn't know what I need."

I told him I had no problem with his taking over the ordering as long as we could maintain certain cost relationships and inventory turn. He said, "Just show me how we can keep track of that."

In a flash, I was largely unemployed! Now that I had more time, I looked around for other opportunities and hit on catering. Actually, it was more like the catering idea hit on me!

Catering
The OTC complex is also the headquarters of the US Olympic Committee and about half the sports in the country, so there were always coaches conferences and other events going on. Catering had been primarily handled by outside vendors because the reputation of OTC foodservice had been so poor.

The sad state of OTC catering became very apparent to me about two days after I arrived when we did a small party for the judo team.

Because I'd been focused on settling into the new job, I hadn't been involved in planning for the event. When I dropped by to check on the setup crew, I was shocked! It looked like something you'd do in your college dorm room freshman year – a totally amateur effort.

I still remember seeing a bag of chips lying on the bar. I asked the setup person where the basket was and got a blank stare!

When I suggested we could put the chips in a basket, he got excited! "Wow," he said, "that would really be neat!" At that stage of the game, it appeared that formal catering was taking the Doritos out of the bag!

I saw catering as an opportunity – not only to save money for the sponsoring organizations, but to break up the routine and provide a creative outlet for my kitchen crew. The problem was that I knew little or nothing about catering.

I asked a superb caterer I knew from San Francisco to give us all a bit of direction. We took what he taught us and developed a catering program so good that it eliminated any desire for outside vendors!

Passing the Baton
I ran the parties for a year and a half before I started getting bored. I asked one of my supervisors if she'd like to take over the program. She said she'd love to, but she didn't understand all the details of what to do.

I suggested that she work closely with me for a couple of months. Once she understood what I was doing **and why it made sense to me to do it that way,** she was on her own and could do anything she wanted. Once she was up to speed, I gave her the job. She went off and did things I'd never thought of! I was blown away!

I continued to handle the catering bookings until one day I realized that, too, was unproductive. I was just taking the information from the sponsor and relaying it to the kitchen.

I asked my head chef if he'd prefer to handle the bookings directly and he said it would really be easier. "Often the sponsor asks us a question and we don't know what you told them." So I gave away the bookings, too.

At the end of my time with the Olympics, I was getting rave reviews on parties I didn't even know we did!

In nearly five years at the OTC, I effectively gave my job away at least three times. Each period of "unemployment" allowed me to see possibilities that moved the department into new and exciting directions ... and kept my own interest and enthusiasm high!

Flying Solo

After I passed the baton on catering, some of my colleagues observed that often there were major parties going on and I wasn't there. Because their model of management didn't allow for that, they concluded that I just didn't care. They were so wrong!

I cared intensely, but I cared enough to give them a chance to find out how good they were without me second-guessing them. That's the only way they'd ever really solo. If they needed me, they knew I'd be there as soon as they called, but it was up to them to make the call.

Had I been there, even just to eyeball the layout, I'm sure the crew would have deferred all decisions to me and never really discovered how capable they really were.

When I first got to the OTC, I'd get calls at night and on the weekends. (Certainly if the place is on fire, I want to be perhaps the *second* call they make!) But most of the calls were pretty routine.

When they'd call, I might say, "If I was at a movie and you couldn't reach me, do you have any idea what you would do?" They usually responded that they did. So I'd say, "You're closer to the issue than I am. Give your plan a try and see how it works. We'll talk about it Monday." After I'd done that a few times, they stopped calling.

Your staff already knows what to do when they call you – the only reason they're calling is to cover their butts!

If you have a tendency to yell at people when they do it "wrong" (different than the way you would have done it), you can count on them to ask for – and wait for – your approval before they take any independent action. That will really slow down the operation and make the place a lot harder to manage. If you have the courage to give them the autonomy they crave, you will all learn valuable lessons.

36
How Rules are Made

The odds are you're living with behavior today that resulted directly from some long-forgotten incident involving a member of your staff who left your employ years ago. You see, every time you chew out one of your crew, you add a new "rule" to your company's unwritten code of conduct.

Nobody likes to be yelled at, so it creates an uncomfortable situation. Since you can count on people to avoid pain, the word will travel fast. Not only will that impact your current staff, but as new people are hired, your veteran workers will tell them, "Make sure you never ..." and they won't.

What was the story behind the flare-up that started this paranoia? In time everyone will forget. Perhaps it was just a simple misunderstanding, a harmless difference of opinion or an isolated incident. Perhaps you were just under stress and overreacted.

In the end, the exact circumstances really don't matter. You blew your top about something and the "rule" resulting from that upset will continue to be passed along.

This new "rule" will never show up in your operations manual and it's unlikely that any of your staff will ever discuss it with you. (After all, *you're* the one who so clearly expressed your disapproval, so it's obvious how you feel about it!)

Still, the fallout from the incident will influence everyone's behavior for years. So be careful what you say and how you say it. Be alert for rumors and potential misunderstandings. If you even suspect something is being taken out of context, address it immediately.

If you make a mess, clean it up. If you make a mistake, just do what you'd want your staff to do when one of *them* makes a mistake – admit it, apologize, learn from it, and move on.

Better yet, conduct yourself in such a way that your actions can't be misinterpreted. Always model the behavior you want to see from your staff. Keep your temper. Listen. Watch your tone of voice. Reward progress instead of punishing lapses.

Conduct your counseling sessions in private and never when you're angry. As much as possible, create standards of performance rather than rules. When you expect the best and don't jump to knee-jerk conclusions, everyone feels more respected.

It's all a human equation, after all.

37
Sound Familiar?

To reinforce my previous point, here's an amazing bit of trivia concerning an experiment with shaping behavior in apes. I doubt you'll be training too many primates (although some days it may seem like it!), but see if there's anything in here that strikes a chord:

Start with a cage containing five apes. In the cage, hang a banana on a string and put a set of steps under it. Before long, one of the apes will start to climb toward the banana. As the ape touches the steps, spray all the apes in the cage with cold water. They hate that.

After awhile, when another ape makes an attempt, spray all the apes with cold water again. Quickly the apes realize that if any of them approaches the steps, all of them will be sprayed with cold water! Now you can put the hose away.

Later, if any other ape tries to climb the steps, the remaining apes will try to stop him, even though no cold water is sprayed on them.

Now, remove one ape from the cage and replace it with a new one. The new ape will see the banana and try to climb the steps.

To his horror, all of the others will attack him! After another attempt and attack, he learns that if he makes a move toward the stairs, he'll be assaulted. He'll never try it again.

Then replace another of the original five apes. The newest ape will go to the steps and be attacked. The previous newcomer will take part in the punishment with enthusiasm, even though he had never been sprayed with the cold water.

Replace a third original ape with a new one. The new ape makes it to the steps and is attacked as well. Two of the four apes that beat him have no idea why they weren't permitted to get the banana or why they beat on the newest ape, but that won't stop their participation.

After replacing the fourth and fifth original apes, all the apes that had once been sprayed with cold water will be gone, yet none of the new apes will ever approach the steps.

Why? "Because that's the way it's done around here!"

The lesson: group behavior tends to perpetuate and reinforce itself, even in the absence of direct consequences.

What behavior exists around your place that's no longer supported by either necessity or the expressed desires of management?

Where such behavior exists, what do you plan to do about it?

38
Lazy People

Do you have any lazy people in your organization? If so, treasure them! Lazy people will always figure out how to get things done with the least possible work!

I just love lazy people. They can find ways to do a job in half the time it would take anyone else! This almost sounds silly, but it's true. After all, why would spend twenty hours doing something if it could be done just as well in twelve?

(Because that's the way you have always done it?)

Taking advantage of your staff's natural tendency to do as little work as possible requires a high degree of respect for their innate intelligence. It also takes clear standards, a focus on results and a willingness to let things happen in a different way than you would have done it.

In short, you must we willing to get your results their way1

It doesn't sound too difficult when you look at it like this. After all, your job isn't to do it, just to see that it gets done.

39
Moving the Company

To simplify your life and move your company forward, it helps to understand a little more about thought.

When it comes to thought, all most people are aware of is the **content** – good thoughts are better than bad thoughts. Program your mind with happy thoughts and you'll have a happy life.

That misses the point.

The important point is not **what** you are thinking but **how** you are thinking. Let's explore two distinct modes (ways) of thought.

Memory Mode

One mode of thinking is busy-minded and memory-based. Your memory is like a database containing everything that's ever happened in your life (and what you made up to explain it!) It's all the things your Mom told you that you believed and all the things you learned (or decided for yourself) in church, in school and on the playground.

Your memory contains all the experiences of your life. It's essentially what has been programmed into the database of your in-head computer. You can retrieve anything that's in there, but the data may or may not correlate to any current situation. It's all old stuff!

Memory has its place. In repetitive situations where all the variables are known, memory-based thinking is very helpful. If you didn't have access to memory, every day you'd have to re-learn how to drive a car or how to run your computer. You'd even have to re-learn your kids' names every day (... and they like it when you remember!)

When you're in the memory mode, you actively search the database for information. It's a bearing-down type of activity. When you're in memory mode, you can become very attached to your thoughts.

Solving problems in the memory mode is a process of analysis – you re-sort and re-arrange old data, looking for new answers. If you've ever found yourself repeating patterns in your life or had a feeling of "been there, done that," you have experienced busy-minded thinking – you were caught up in your memory, recycling old ideas.

Helpful as it sometimes is, busy-minded thinking isn't much help when you're faced with situations where all of the variables are *not* known.

When you try to deal with new situations in the memory mode, you must try to interpret new events based on what you know from old events. This only keeps you stuck in the past, repeating old patterns and making the same old mistakes.

In any situation involving another person, all the variables are never known, so if you rely on memory when dealing with others, it's likely to create problems.

When you deal with new information in a busy-minded way, either the information is in your database or it's not. If you find a parallel in memory, the other person is "right." If you can't find a compatible bit of data, then the other person is "wrong!"

If I jump to a conclusion about what you mean as soon as you start to talk – if I think, "Oh, I know where this is going" – then I've missed it entirely. I'm drawing conclusions about you based on things in my past that didn't have anything to do with you!

Now let's look at another mode of thought:

Reflective Mode
The other mode of thought is reflective thinking. It's sometimes called receiver mode thinking because, unlike the memory mode where you speed up and actively search for answers in your mental database, reflective thinking is a process of slowing down and allowing the answers to come to you.

95

This is the most appropriate mode of thinking when faced with situations where all the variables are not known (which is most of the issues managers deal with on a daily basis.)

Reflective thinking is more like standing by a gently flowing river watching ideas float past on the current. You notice them with curiosity, but don't become attached to what you see. When you see something that looks appropriate, you just pluck it out.

The reflective mode is the realm of common sense. (Common sense isn't directly tied to personal experience, is it?) It's the realm of perspective, where you suddenly see a bigger picture. It's also the realm of insight. When you spend most of your time in this mode, most people will see it as wisdom.

I suspect you've probably experienced the reflective mode of thinking a few times yourself. This is the quiet mind we spoke of in Chapter 12.

Reflective thinking is clear-minded thought. When your mind quiets down, you will automatically tap into a flow of wisdom far deeper than anything you can access consciously.

Some may call it women's intuition or a strong hunch, but it's really just quietly watching ideas float by and recognizing the ones that apply to the situation at hand.

Good and Bad?
The two modes of thinking are not mutually exclusive. When your mind is quiet, you have instant access to anything stored in your memory. If something in your past experience is relevant, it will immediately occur to you, but you don't go into a new situation burdened with old ideas that don't necessarily apply to the situation at hand.

It's not that memory is bad and reflection is good – there's an appropriate place for each. Healthy psychological functioning, in fact, is defined as the appropriate use of both the memory and reflective modes of thinking.

Problems and Conditions

I said earlier that a problem is only a situation where the solution has not yet occurred to you and that a condition is a situation that can't be changed. How can you tell the difference? Just clear your mind, tap into that reflective mode of thinking and wait for the obvious answer to occur to you as an insight.

You will learn more, create a more positive climate and move your company farther when you deal with others from a quiet mind. In that state, you are not judgmental of others' ideas, your thoughts are fresh and you will see possibilities all around

Most people have had the experience of stumbling across quiet-minded insights, but the idea that you can actually function from there is a new – and I hope intriguing – possibility.

40
Columbo Management

When you can maintain a quiet mind while dealing with others, you operate in a state of mild puzzlement ... a lot like Peter Falk's character in the old TV series "Columbo."

You have no pre-conceived ideas about situations, make no judgements, and don't automatically assume you know what others really mean by the words they use.

To others, it can look like you're "dumb as dirt," but that's a good thing. "I don't know" is a very powerful place to operate from.

When you "know," it's very easy to stop listening, to ignore other possibilities because you already "know." When this happens, you just look arrogant and pig-headed. (Did you ever work for somebody like this?)

But when a staff member says, "What should I do?" and your first response is, "I don't know. Let's look at this for a second," it will slow your mind down. You'll tend to ask more and better questions and you're likely to receive new and unexpected information.

You will avoid most misunderstandings by not jumping to conclusions and taking time to consider other points of view. You will always learn something new. Ultimately you'll do less work because your staff will become more involved in the process.

Your goal is to get comfortable with the idea of not knowing. In fact, you actually try to not "know" very much at all. The less you think you know, the quieter your mind becomes and the greater the possibilities you'll see.

The more you become at ease with the idea that you really don't need to know everything (and feel terrific that you don't), the more you'll live in this quiet, insightful state.

When you think about it, everything you "know" is really just old stuff – it has already happened. Past experience has value, but it doesn't apply to every set of circumstances.

The only real way to know if past experience may be relevant to a present situation is to keep your mind quiet, gather more current information and wait for an insight. That process starts with "I don't know" and a healthy curiosity. Do you see how easily it works?

Robert Kausen put it this way:

> *"People might find it helpful to think of "I don't know" as the button you press to access deeper creativity. The "Know It All" accesses data banks of old information. The humility required to go into the "I don't know mode" (the unknown) instantly calls on our deeper creative resources to see something new.*
>
> *(Our egos tend to hate this, but then when did the ego ever come up with anything new and insightful?)*
>
> *It takes some courage initially to get comfortable with the feeling of free-falling in the unknown. Still, the results of spending more and more time in that centered, creative flow of our innate, healthy thinking are well worth it."*

This doesn't mean everything you know is wrong, it just suggests there's always more information than you have and to be sure you are certain about what's actually happening before taking action.

To illustrate, say a bartender comes to you all bent out of shape. "I've got a guy at the bar who is causing a lot of trouble," he snaps. What should I do?" At that point you don't have enough information to even begin to answer the question.

If you respond, "I don't know. What exactly is he doing?" you might find out enough to be able to make a better suggestion, to ask a more intelligent question ... or to help the bartender discover that he already knows how to handle it without you.

For example, asking, "What did you say to him and how did he respond?" will give you a clearer understanding of the situation ... and keep the responsibility for a solution with the bartender where it belongs.

No two people see things the same way. Your cashier may think the sky is falling when she runs out of tape in the cash register! You would do well to ask more questions before you have a knee jerk reaction and call for a particular course of action.

(By the way, "I don't know" isn't the best response in every situation. If the building is on fire, the appropriate action is to have everyone evacuate the premises immediately!)

When I initiated a discussion of "I don't know" in my weekly e-letter, I received a number of great responses. Here are several which shed even more light on this notion:

Paula:

This is a very important lesson to learn. Many people don't think it's OK to say "I don't know". They think people want an answer, even if they have to make one up. However, I find that saying it slow me down and allows me to think a little more clearly.

Several years ago I went through a personal transformation, realizing I didn't have to be perfect or know it all. I started saying "I don't know" more and more. It really did liberate me from having to be all-knowing. I don't always remember to use this technique, but I do find it helpful.

Vince:

"I don't know" happens to be one of my favorite answers. You really nailed this one! Not only have I worked for people like that, I've had too many employees like that. It takes a long time to get people to understand that it's OK to say "I don't know" when it's the truth.

Sometimes "I don't know" is the right answer. I'm often surprised at how smart and self-confident people can sound when they answer a question with "I don't know" and how shallow and insecure they seem when they try to bluff an answer.

Gene:

Thanks for the comment on staff bringing questions without solutions or recommendations. They assume that, "Gene will know the answer, let's ask him" without doing any soul-searching or research.

For some of my staff, it's an easy way to get their work done ... get someone else (me!) to do it!

Sometimes I fall into the trap by coming up with an answer without first asking, "What do you think?" It's always assumed the Boss knows, so they just ask – and sometimes the Boss thinks he should know so he responds – with an answer that may be less than perfect. Not good.

When your mind is quiet and you're slightly puzzled, you'll tend to ask more probing questions – questions that will occur naturally to you in the moment. You'll be awash in fresh ideas.

By admitting you don't know the answer, it takes the pressure of time and accountability away. Sure, I know many answers but not all of them ... and I shouldn't be expected to know it all, right?

Remember, your job isn't to **have** the answers, just to be able to **find** the answers – and the best answers often come from other people ... if you give them the opportunity.

[Note: In my experience, the more certain you are that you're "right," the more likely it is that you're totally out to lunch! At the least, the odds are great that insisting on your opinion at that point won't give you the results you want.]

41
Lists

I'm sure you have a to-do list ... and it's easy to think that working the list will move the company forward. Let's look at that idea:

First, think about what sort of thought to-do lists typically represent. Usually busy-minded thinking, right? ("I've got to do this, I've got to do that.") What kind of thinking moves the company forward? Quiet-minded thinking, of course.

So how do you reconcile the two?

Let me share another story to illustrate. This one also involves my late friend Mark Sneed of Phillips Seafood. In addition to five multi-million dollar restaurants, Mark was also responsible for Phillips' seafood plants and retail operations around the world. He was a busy, brilliant man who increased his company's sales by over 60% in just two years.

The other player in this short story is one of Mark's managers – also a talented operator but a man wedded to his to-do list. Given a choice between his Day Timer and his left arm, he'd keep the book! He got results, but always seemed to be in a rush. Does that sound familiar?

Mark and I gave him a hard time about his list fixation but he never quite grasped what we were trying to help him see.

I recall the last time we tried to make the point. The three of us were at lunch and Mark was talking about how to make progress. He said, "Every once in awhile I have a list day. Yesterday was like that for me. There were a lot of things I just had to do so I made my list and spent the day working on it."

"At the end of the day I had handled most of the things on my list, but I didn't move the company anywhere yesterday. All I did was get the things on my list done."

He went on, "I move the company when I don't have a list, when my mind is quiet and I can see possibilities. I move the company when I can see things that we could be doing or where we might be creating a problem for ourselves." Think about it.

Where's the Problem?
Lists themselves aren't a problem, but relying on lists can create one if you think you're making progress by ticking everything off the list.

Don't confuse being busy with being productive.

There's even value in lists that come from a busy mind. In any business, there are always things that need to be done and writing them all down can help keep your mind uncluttered. I use lists to free my mind from the need to remember trivial tasks.

The key lies in what happens to them once they appear on the list. Just because something makes it onto your list doesn't mean that you're the only person who can – or should – do the work.

It's possible to create a list from a quiet mind. When you're struck with an insight, write it down, get quiet again and wait for another aha." Put these insights together and you'll have a very powerful plan of action. In fact, if you don't write down your insights when they strike you, they're likely to slip away again.

Here are some better questions to ask yourself about your list:

Does this Have to Be Done at All?
What would happen if this item wasn't addressed? You'll be amazed at the number of things we do because we've always done them, but that wouldn't affect our business at all if they weren't done.

Who's the Best Person to Do This?
If its something that must be done, the next thing to determine is who's the best person to do it? Determine whose performance is most affected and whose behavior has to change and assign the task to them.

Is It a High-Return Activity?

High-return activities are things you probably should do yourself. These include bringing in new business, organizing or energizing the staff and sponsoring charitable events – projects that move the company into new areas.

You can safely delegate low-return activities like scheduling, creating contests, ordering and inventories. Even most staff hiring is something your crew can safely handle with a little coaching. (If you give people the opportunity, they won't hire jerks. After all, they'll have to work with them!)

Much of what we take on is only because we've become attached to the idea that it's our job or that we're the only ones who can do it right ... then we wonder why our staff is so inept and we don't have any free time for ourselves.

Every time you do a job that someone on your staff is capable of doing, you deprive them of an opportunity to learn. At the same time, you're not learning anything new, so nobody benefits.

All the day-to-day mechanics of running the place are activities that someone else on the team can do or can learn how to do. Get busy. Get routine tasks off your plate as quickly as you can. They only clutter your mind and keep you from seeing the possibilities that will move your company forward.

42
Stress

Do you feel stress as a normal part of being out there on the planet? Since stress on the job seems to be a fact of life for many hospitality managers, it deserves a closer look.

We have funny ideas about stress. There's "stress management" and some people think a certain amount of stress is good for you. Insanity! Once you understand where stress really comes from, you can decide for yourself whether you want it in your life or not.

My favorite swamp philosopher, Pogo, put it very nicely when he said, "We have met the enemy and he is us." When it comes to stress, nobody is doing it to you except you. That may sound a little strange, so I'll give you an analogy that I think may help. It's a golf analogy but you don't have to be a golfer to understand it.

A Relaxing Day of Golf?
It's a gorgeous day and you're going to play golf. You get up on the first tee, look down the fairway and think, "200 yards, just left of center." You line up the shot and whack that ball ... thirty yards into the trees!

So you jump in the cart and head down the fairway – 200 yards just left of center – to get your ball, because that's where it's supposed to be. You look all around for it, but it's nowhere to be found.

At first, you're a bit confused, then you get irritated, then you really get mad. "Where's my #@!% ball? It's supposed to be right here! Somebody's head is going to roll for this!" You throw a tantrum in the middle of the golf course because your ball is not where it's "supposed" to be. Basically a pretty stupid move, right?

It won't move the ball to that spot, the flow of the game stops, you look like a jerk and nobody wants to play with you anymore!

This is easy to see in golf – the ball is in the trees, go into the trees and play the ball! It's how the game works.

Obvious in golf, perhaps, but how many times in your life have you done something that was "supposed" to produce a certain result, then gone to where that result was "supposed" to be and thrown a tantrum because it wasn't there?

It won't produce the result, the flow of the game stops, you look like a jerk and nobody wants to play with you anymore!

When the game is on, the only option you have is to play the ball!

The fact that you wanted the ball to be somewhere other than where it ended up is interesting, but has about as much relevance to the game as the color of your golf shirt!

This doesn't mean you have to play out of the trees forever.

When the game is over, take a lesson!

When the game is over, see the golf pro for some advice on your swing ... but when the game is on, you have no choice but to play the ball wherever it lies.

Here's where it gets interesting.

Can you see that "200 yards just left of center" is just a thought? You made it up. You could've said "thirty yards into the trees" and saved yourself a lot of grief!

It's not a problem to stand on the first tee and think "200 yards just left of center" – it's only when you get attached to that thought that you start to create difficulty for yourself.

Think about it. You made it up, you got attached to it and then you got angry when it didn't happen. Who's the villain here? Who's doing the thinking?

If you weren't attached to where the ball went, you could shoot 300 and have a great day! (Personally, I think for what a round of golf costs, you should get in as many strokes as you can!) But if you get it into your mind that the day is a total bust if don't shoot an 80 – and it's not happening – you have a miserable time.

In the end, the ball is still going into the cup, it's just going to happen a little differently than the way you originally thought it would. Is this really a problem? Is it worth selling your peace of mind for?

The stress factors in our lives are just thoughts that we make up, then get attached to ... and there are a lot of them:

"If you really cared, you would ..."
"This shouldn't be happening ..."
"It isn't right that ..."
"We need more time to ..."
"This all has to be done by ..."
"You have no cause to ..."

Who said so?

As in the golfing example, you had a thought, you got attached to it and then you got stressed out when it didn't happen. The fact that you had the thought doesn't automatically make it valid or relevant.

The only truth is that things aren't playing out the way you made them up. (Do they ever?) Get over it. Once you can see stress as just a product of your own thinking, you have the power to do something about it.

Your level of stress goes down because you lose your tolerance for feeling stressed. As you spend more time with a quiet mind, it will feel like fingernails on the blackboard when your thinking gets speeded up, you start chasing your tail and get caught in your own ideas of how things "ought to" be.

When the game is on, let go of your pre-determined ideas of how you wanted it to be, accept things where they lie and play on from there. Your stress will disappear and life will get much easier.

We'll look at this again in Chapter 43.

43
Warning Signs

You can tell when you're starting to get caught in your own thinking because you'll feel irritation, stress or even anger. You'll start thinking in terms of "should" and "shouldn't," or "right" and "wrong." Your thoughts will become more negative and judgmental. Your body will tense up.

Learn to recognize the signs and take them for what they are – signals that you're starting to breathe your own exhaust.

If you find yourself thinking ill of your kids, your mate, your staff or what's happening in your life, recognize that it's just a thought – another bubble from the bubble machine. It doesn't mean anything.

Let go of the thought and it will have no impact. Get attached to it and it will make your life miserable.

When you sense a warning sign, ask yourself, "Is the game on?" If the game is on, play the ball. If the game is over, take a lesson.

For example, if you're in the middle of the rush and discover you're out of a critical item, throwing a tantrum won't produce that item. Play the ball. Think, "How can I make this work without that item?"

When the rush is over, take a lesson – look at why you ran out and see what you can do to keep it from happening again.

That's the way it works in business. That's the way it works in your life. Stress is a choice, something you do to yourself.

Why would you do that to you?

44
Pre-Determined Ideas

People, particularly people under pressure, have a tendency to resist any suggestion that's at odds with their pre-determined idea (PDI) of how things "should be."

For example, let's say you offer a sandwich that includes french fries. In the middle of the lunch rush, an elderly customer asks the waitress if he can substitute a small salad for the fries. Her first reaction may be to say "no" under any or all of the following conditions:

- if she takes the request as an imposition (PDI: customers shouldn't deliberately try to make my day more complicated)
- if the substitution will mean more work to place the order (PDI: customers should understand I don't have time for this right now)
- if she doesn't know how to enter the substitution in the POS system (PDI: customers shouldn't try to confuse me when I am busy)
- if she thinks the patron is just being contrary (PDI: customers should be happy with what's offered on the menu).
- if she thinks that everyone must be treated the same way (PDI: if I let one person do it, I'll have to let everyone do it)

If you had a staff member who behaved in this way – who habitually said "no" as a knee-jerk reaction – you might conclude that they "had an attitude" or weren't service-oriented.

After all, if they can't easily see what's required to accommodate the guest's request, or if they're not willing to consider a new idea and try to handle it, they shouldn't be in the service industry, right?

Where did they ever get such a negative outlook? You would certainly never do anything like that ... or would you?

In the interests of introspection, let's say you're in the middle of your managerial juggling act (trying to build sales up, keep costs down, find good staff, put out fires, have a life and the like) and one of your staff makes a last-minute request for a schedule change.

Your first reaction might well be to say "no" under any or all of the following conditions:

- if you take the request as an imposition (PDI: employees shouldn't deliberately try to make my day more complicated)
- if the substitution will mean more work to rearrange the schedule (PDI: the staff should know I don't have time for this right now)
- if you don't know how you're going to be able to accommodate the change (PDI: the staff shouldn't try to confuse me when I'm busy)
- if you think that the staff member is being contrary (PDI: employees should be happy with the schedule the way it was originally written)
- if you think that everyone must be treated the same way (PDI: if I let one person do it, I'll have to let everyone do it)

Do you see what I mean? This is just an illustration of how easily you can get caught in your own thinking and how it's reflected in the behavior of your staff.

How it "Should Be"
In both these examples, the problem grows out of pre-determined ideas – something one person has decided in advance *should* go a certain way.

We all do this and there's no fault in merely having the thought. The difficulty comes when you become attached to your idea of how things *should* be and either try to force it to happen that way or resist when it is playing out in a different manner.

Your idea of how things "should" be is only a thought. Somebody told you something and you believed them or you just got attached to some idea in your head. Who said your idea was true? When you give your own thoughts more weight than they deserve, you can get in a lot of trouble.

Role Models
So what does all this have to do with the real world of business? As a start, it may help you make course corrections with your staff.

For example, if your crew seems focused on what they *can't* do for your guests (as opposed to thinking about what they *can* do), make very sure you are not, in fact, guilty of exactly the same behavior.

Interestingly, getting the staff to say "yes" starts with the attitude and actions of management. What *they* see is what *you* will get.

Do you roll your eyes and think, "what a jerk" when someone on your staff behaves in a certain way? Your behavior toward your crew in the daily course of business provides the model for how your staff will behave when one of your patrons makes a "stupid request" or does something they "shouldn't" have done.

See how often you can have phrases like these be the first words from your lips, particularly when something unexpected comes up:

"Of course we can!"
"It would be my pleasure."
"That will be no problem at all."
"I never thought of that."
"What an interesting idea!"

You are always the role model whether you want the job or not!

45
Start to Notice

Start to notice your own tendency to resist anything that's at odds with *your* pre-determined ideas of how things are "supposed to be."

Lighten Up
Start to notice when you look for something wrong any time a staff member shows initiative and does something differently than the way you would have done it.

Watch Yourself
Start to notice your reaction when a staff member asks for something outside the normal routine, like a last-minute schedule change. Again, you're the role model. How you handle it will be imitated.

Relax
Start to notice any thought that contains a "should" or a "supposed to" and be wary of it. When your brain bubbles up a "should" idea, just let it pass. Don't allow yourself to take it seriously or get attached to it. It's only a thought and it has no importance other than what you arbitrarily choose to assign it.

Listen
Start to notice what happens when you aren't listening to what other people actually *mean* by what they say. You (and they) can tell when you're not listening because you'll have an answer in your mind before they even stop talking. Don't presume that your personal experiences are applicable to another person's issues.

Learn
Start to accept that other people's actions and requests make sense to them. The fact that they may or may not make sense to you is not required. Seek to understand before deciding what to do.

Open Up

Start to notice what happens if you allow yourself more than a passing thought that things shouldn't be happening the way they're happening. Notice how judgmental the thought is and how just the thought can paralyze you. Notice how disrespectful and arrogant you seem to others when you think your view of the world is superior to theirs.

Wake Up

Start to notice when your own agenda seems more important than that of the people you're dealing with, be they guests, staff or family. Notice how unserved those people feel when it happens.

In short, notice your pre-determined ideas and don't let them run your life. We all have personal preferences, but imposing your view of the world – your pre-determined ideas – on others is disrespectful. It only preserves the status quo and keeps you from seeing fresh possibilities.

46
Don't Compete, Excel

Every restaurant struggles to increase sales. It doesn't matter if they're a national chain with deep pockets and a smooth format or an independent trying to pursue a dream and carve out a niche.

In either case, many managers seem to spend more and more time worrying about competitors, looking over their shoulders, counting cars and trying to outguess the other guys.

When they ask me what they should do, I tell them they should stop competing – that competing can be dangerous to their professional survival!

Let me explain with another example:

Have you ever been driving down the road and had a police car following you? I don't know about you, but when that happens to me, I find I am suddenly fascinated by my speedometer and paying undue attention to my rear view mirror!

In this condition, I am not as focused on what I'm doing! The closer eye I keep on the cop, the higher my anxiety level rises and I'm more prone to silly mistakes. I am definitely not as good a driver when I'm paying too much attention to who or what is behind me!

The same dynamic applies in business. When you're fixated on what the competition is doing, it drains vital energy away from your primary focus which should be on running the very best business you can.

An obsession with your competitors can cause you to make silly mistakes. Paying too much attention to what others are doing can interfere with giving your own guests a consistently memorable time!

Wake up!

Be competitive ... but don't compete. Know what your major competitors are doing but don't become obsessive about it. You can't prosper by doing what they're doing – you can only thrive by doing what *you* do better than anyone else can do it.

Monetary success and personal joy will come when your sole concern – your driving passion – is how you can excel!

47
Tone of Voice

A final insight into dealing with people is this: the message you send is not communicated by your choice of words. **The message you deliver is always in the *feeling* behind the tone of voice you use.**

Your words, while important, are only a vehicle that carries the emphasis, inflections and feelings bearing the message that others receive.

You can probably recall an incident in which someone said one thing to you but conveyed a totally different message by the way they said it. Which message did you believe?

Everyone makes assumptions, forms judgments and draws conclusions from another's tone of voice.

If you've ever watched a foreign language film or been in a country where you didn't speak the language, you probably still had a pretty good sense of what was happening, even if you couldn't discern all the details. Body language and tone of voice communicate a lot.

The typical manager's day can be hectic. As the pace picks up, it's easy to forget the importance of voice tone when dealing with others. Under pressure you can easily snap off a harsh answer or react in a way that delivers a message totally at odds with the one contained in your words.

If you speak to people in a disrespectful tone, you'll get a negative reaction. If you speak in a pleading tone, people won't take you seriously. Either extreme hampers productivity.

A neutral tone of voice will automatically foster an adult relationship between you and your staff which will, in turn, improve the work climate.

In a higher climate, your team will be naturally inclined to provide exceptional service to your guests, feel more involved in their work and identify more closely with your business.

To help make sure your intonation matches your intention when you're talking with someone, pause before speaking. Take a deep breath, clear your head of any distracting thoughts and allow yourself to connect with the other person. Then simply say what you need to say.

Good communication starts with cleaning up your internal state – a process that is quite natural. When you become aware of your distractions, you automatically start the process of self-correction.

You will be surprised and pleased by how clear your communication will become, how infrequently little misunderstandings will arise and how effective you'll become at human relations.

"Follow a trail of bold mistakes and at
the end of them you will find a genius."
– Roy H. Williams

Part 4

Yeah, But ...

"When the best leaders' work is done,
the people say 'We did it ourselves.'"
– Lao Tzu

48
Getting Acclimated

When the common sense of these principles first struck me and I saw a way out of my world of weeds, I didn't know for sure if it was even possible to run a business the way I'm suggesting in this book. After all, I'd spent my entire career up to that point getting quite good at trying to force things to happen.

What I *was* certain of, however, was that kicking butt, taking names and working 80+ hours a week was no longer my idea of a good time.

Once I saw it, this new vision was the only approach that made sense to me. I figured if I couldn't run a restaurant this way, I'd sell auto parts! My peace of mind had become more important to me than my ability to work myself into an early grave.

What I wasn't prepared for was how incredibly effective it was.

I got results in six months that I would have been thrilled to accomplish in six years by any standard I ever had ... and I never talked to my staff about any of the things I've covered in this book.

At the time I just didn't have any words for it. But **the fact that it had shifted for me was enough to change the whole organization!**

However, I had some questions when I first started down this new road and I suspect you may have a few as well.

In the next few chapters, I will address several of the more common areas that people seem to have trouble grasping as they make the move into this brave new world.

49
Out to Lunch

You may have gathered that when you're having a bad day, that's a great time to disappear into the office and do paperwork rather than wandering around and bringing down the mood of the entire operation.

However, there are only so many times you can tell the boss, "Well, I felt a little off track so I went out to play golf." He may suggest you look for a new job at the golf club!

So what do you do when you're a little "out to lunch" and still must perform? Here are a few suggestions that may help decide what to do:

Can You Live With It?
When you're off track, the tendency is to feel that you must take action immediately. Do you really have to do something immediately ... or could it wait until you're seeing things more clearly? If so, put it off.

Recognize Your State of Mind
If you can't delay action until a better time, the best thing you can do is to realize that you're a little "out to lunch" and aren't seeing things quite clearly. Don't trust your perceptions – everything will look like a disaster when you're in a low mood.

Listen
The fastest way to regain your perspective and innate wisdom is to quiet your mind, realize you don't have a clue ... and listen. Listen with humility. Listen with curiosity, Listen for an insight.

Trust the Process
When the insight strikes you, just follow that idea and it will bring you right back into balance every time.

A Case Study
Let me share a story to illustrate how this process worked for me.

I had an employee, Darryl, who was a real rising star. He was coming on strong and I saw great things ahead for him. But suddenly he started to self-destruct, doing things that I thought were way out of character.

For example, we had slick floors, so we'd issued non-slip shoes to all our crew. Darryl came to work in the middle of a Colorado winter wearing his leather sole dress shoes, slipped, and had a Worker's Comp claim.

I didn't know what was going on, but I knew that I couldn't live with it any longer, so I caught him on a break one day and said, "Darryl, I don't have a clue as to what's going on here." (And I didn't. I didn't even know what I was going to say after I said that!)

That quieted my mind down big time and suddenly an idea struck me, one that had never occurred to me before. I just went with it. "But if I had to guess," I went on, "my guess would be that you really want to get out of this job, but you just can't quite figure out how to do it."

Darryl got a sly little smile on his face and said, "Well you know, you're pretty close." I asked, "What do you want to do?" He replied, "I think I'd better get out of here."

Contrast this approach to the way you might normally deal with a situation like this: ("What's your problem, Darryl? You're better than this!") It's shocking how often we can be so certain about things when we have no real clue about what is really happening.

I'll grant you there's a certain leap of faith in handling things in this manner, but if you don't have a clue, there's no use pretending you do – just quiet your mind and trust that the answer will appear.

It will ... and it'll be right on the money every time!

50
Non-Compliance

Let's say that you want a member of your staff to achieve a certain result and it's just not happening. The old model of management would call for several counseling sessions (properly documented, of course) followed by termination if the person was unable to deliver the desired results.

While termination is sometimes a necessary course of action, it isn't the universal answer to every performance lapse. There are several other possibilities that might explain a lack of compliance and allow you to salvage what would otherwise be a lose-lose situation.

Here are seven possible explanations for the lack of results that I suggest you explore – roughly in the order listed – before you decide to cut an under-performing employee loose:

1. They Don't Understand What You Want
Just because you know the results you're trying to achieve doesn't automatically mean your staff does, so the first step is to be certain they know exactly what you want them to do.

This isn't as easy as it sounds. Lee Cockrell, VP of Walt Disney World once told me that people cannot deliver a higher level of customer service than they have personally experienced. If what he says is true (and I believe it is), does it make sense to fire a person for delivering poor service when they really have no idea what you're talking about?

Start by determining whether or not the employee has a true grasp of what you're asking so you aren't expecting something that's beyond their comprehension, even if (especially if) it seems obvious to you.

2. They Don't Understand Why It's Important
After really listening to the person, if you're certain they know what you want, the next possibility is they don't understand why it's important.

124

In the foodservice industry, sanitation practices can easily fall into this category. "I mean, I get the hand-washing thing, but what's the big deal?" Based on experience, I'd say that many workers, both in service and retail operations, apparently have no understanding of the value of a repeat customer.

Whose fault is that? If you don't tell them, how are they supposed to know? So the next step in resolving performance issues is to educate the staff member on the importance of what you're requesting.

3. They Don't Understand How to Do it

Particularly if you have a tendency to yell at someone when they make a mistake, your staff will never tell you they don't know how to do something you've asked them to do. Nobody likes to be yelled at, so they'll just smile, nod their heads and hope you'll go away.

Here's an example of how that dynamic plays out:

The Mystery of the Mop

I can give you an example from personal experience: At the age of 14, I was hired by a small restaurant on Cape Cod for my first job – washing dishes (by hand!) during the summer tourist season. The training for my frightening new responsibilities was concise and pointed – a single sentence: "Get back there and do it!" This was followed by one sentence of counseling: "If you screw up, you're out of here!" Ah, the world of work!

Like most teenagers in the days before automatic dishwashers, I had lots of dishwashing experience, so that part of the job was pretty easy. But I still remember my terror the first time I was pointed to the cleaning gear and told to mop the floor.

Talk about panic! I'd never seen a string mop in my life! We certainly didn't use one at home so I had no idea what it was or how to use it. My boss had me so terrified of making a mistake that I didn't dare reveal my ignorance by asking him to show me what to do. After all, if I screwed up, I'd be fired!

Fortunately, Manny, one of the breakfast cooks, saw the terror in my eyes and took me under his wing. He realized I was clueless, taught me how to use the mop and patiently worked with me until I had mastered it.

In addition to being my mentor, he also became my inspector, making me re-do anything that didn't meet his standards while making sure I understood why it was important to do it a certain way.

Almost single-handedly, Manny helped me survive my first employment adventure. Thinking back on the experience, it's interesting to realize that I still remember Manny, but the names of the restaurant and that jerk of a boss have long since slipped from my memory.

The lesson here is that just because *you* know how to do something doesn't mean that everybody else on the planet does. You'd do well to ascertain the facts before taking more radical action.

4. It Doesn't Have to Be Done!

If things are still not happening, the next possibility could be that it really doesn't make any difference in the daily operation whether the task is done or not!

Admittedly, this is seldom the case, but too often we do things just "because we've always done them." At the OTC, I eliminated two days of counting, pricing and extending food inventories once I learned that nobody ever did anything with the figures!

5. They Have a Better Way to Do it

If the task needs to be done and you've covered the what, why and how, the next possibility is they're not doing it your way because they have a better way to do it!

(This might be a good time to re-read the discussion about the value of lazy people in Chapter 37.)

You can avoid this trap by focusing on results rather than activities. If you're getting the results you want and no laws are being broken, who cares if one of your workers does it differently than you would?

When you define results rather than activities, you allow people to interpret their jobs in a way that works for them ... and that will always improve both retention and productivity.

6. They Can't Do it

The next possibility is that they just can't do it – physically or mentally it's simply beyond their capabilities. This doesn't necessarily make them incompetent, it just means they've been mis-cast.

If you put a "numbers person" in a customer contact position or place a "people person" in a job where they have no interaction with others, you're very likely to see performance problems.

As in the example of Chris the dishwasher, just because someone isn't good at one job doesn't mean they couldn't excel in another.

7. They Won't Do it

If you're comfortable all the possibilities above have been consider and you're still not getting the performance you need, the only othe explanation is that the person just won't do what you need done.

In that case, do yourself and the employee a favor and "free up their future" to pursue another line of work! Everyone is good at something but not everybody is good at what you need done.

Given how difficult it is to find and retain quality staff, termination should be the option of last choice. Don't give up on anyone until you've given them every opportunity to succeed.

51
reeing up the Future

...tarted working from this understanding, I had a staff
...ber who wasn't performing up to my standards. If I could have
become angry, I could have fired her, but I knew she was doing the best
she could. Still, I wasn't getting the needed performance and she wasn't
a good fit elsewhere in the company. I had to do something ... but what?

How Bad Can You Get?
By way of background, I
must confess that I was
never very good at firing
people. How bad? When
I was running a hotel in
the Virgin Islands, I did
such a bad job of firing
one of my staff that the
entire crew walked out in

protest and someone came back in the middle of the night to sabotage
the water system in the condos!

(In self-defense, I should point out that I was working 120 hours a week
and was totally brain dead, but that's no excuse.)

In contrast, if I fired twenty people in the course of my 4½ years at the
Olympics – and I probably did – nineteen of them thanked me! I was
stunned!

Based on my application of the principles we have discussed, here is my
format for letting someone go:

Can You Live with It?
If you can, keep coaching. The question is less about whether they **can**
do the job than it is about whether they **will** do the job. This is the time
to explore all the possibilities discussed in the previous chapter.

Respect the Power of Timing

If you can't live with it, pick your moment as best you can. Understand there's a time when people can hear you and there's a time when they can't. If you've just had a major upset on the job, this isn't the best moment to have a serious discussion about someone's future with the company. If you can, take a break and deal with it when everyone is in a more receptive mood.

Maintain a No-Fault Perspective

Understand that it's not their fault. They asked for a job and you gave it to them. Everyone tried their best but it just didn't work. You don't need a "bad guy." In fact, looking for one will only make things worse.

Operate from Respect

Just because someone failed to meet your performance standards doesn't make them a screw-up. Everyone is really good at something, but this just wasn't it! Respect is a key factor in keeping the exchange on a positive level.

Be Clear and Direct

Don't beat around the bush. Get to the point, say what you have to say and cut the cord quickly with certainly. It'll be less painful (and more respectful) for everyone.

Clean it Up and Move On

If you make a mess, take responsibility for cleaning it up and get on with your life. All you can do is the best you can do in the moment. It won't necessarily go smoothly every time.

Adios, Harry

To illustrate, let's say that it's time to let Harry go. You've worked with him and worked with him and it's just not happening. There's nowhere else in the operation where he can fit in and you're out of ideas. Pick your moment as best you can and ask to see Harry in private.

The scene might play out roughly like this:

"Harry, this isn't working. You know it and I know it ... and it's frustrating to me. I'm sure that if I was more skillful, we might have found a way to make it work, but I've tried everything I can think of ... and I know you have, too. There are too many other demands on my time and I can't spend any more time on this. You're going to have to find something else."

129

Nineteen times out of twenty, they said, "Well, you're right," and we parted on good terms. I did have one person go ballistic, but the results were still far better than I'd ever achieved before.

My point is that it doesn't have to take much longer or be any more complicated than this. The fact that it isn't working shouldn't come as a surprise to anyone and you won't do the Harrys in your life (or yourself) any favors by dragging out the inevitable.

Notice that the approach is direct, respectful and leaves no room for negotiation. If you come across as less than certain about the action you're taking, you'll get an argument every time.

Take charge of the meeting, do what you need to do and if you make a mess, clean it up and move on.

You won't be right every time, but the truth is – or certainly should be – that you both gave it your best effort and it just didn't work.

I can look back on some of the people I let go at the OTC and see a few possibilities now that I missed back then. It's a humbling realization, but all you can do is the best you can do at the time.

52
Reaching Agreement

You'll find your professional (and personal) life will get easier as you learn to be guided by these principles. Becoming a better listener and opening up to the ideas of your staff will take you into exciting new realms, but I'm not advocating management by committee.

The final call and ultimate responsibility for decisions still lies with management ... and realistically, you won't always be in complete agreement with your staff on everything.

To keep peace in the family, it's not really necessary to put every decision up to a vote or have somebody win and somebody lose each time. You'll still want to proceed as smoothly as possible, so here's a format that can help you reach agreement when you find yourself at odds with another person:

Establish a Climate for a Meeting of the Minds
The first step in reaching agreement is be sure you're setting yourself up to succeed. Consider these items as you get started:

Respect the Power of Timing
Pick your moment. Find a time when the person isn't distracted by business pressure and can focus on the task at hand.

Recognize the Power of a Supportive Atmosphere
Rapport is the lubricant of agreement – don't leave home without it! If you can't reach a point of feeling comfortable together you'll never reach a meaningful accord, so take the time for some small talk to "plug in" with each other before proceeding.

If you lose that personal connection, nothing good is likely to come of pushing on. Take a break, let everyone clear their heads and continue. If you are unable to re-establish rapport, it's best to end the meeting and try again later.

To those who are anxious to "get on with it," this may seem like wasting time, but in the long run it will greatly shorten the time it takes to reach a true meeting of the minds.

Listen for Insights

Have you noticed how often thoughtful listening pops up as a key skill in enlightened management?

You want to listen for the content, of course, but it's also important to listen for insights, meaning and understanding. The other person's position makes sense to them and it will definitely help you to understand what they want (and why) before you press ahead.

Until the other parties feel that you truly understand where they're coming from, they will be fixated on trying you get you to see their point of view. You don't need to agree, disagree or express an opinion, just understand why they see things the way they do.

When you listen for insights, you don't really know *what* you're listening for ... but you'll recognize it when you hear it.

Work from Agreement

Once you've established a strong connection, the next step is to start establishing agreement. Each point you can agree on will deepen the connection and raise the climate between you. As the climate improves, items that once looked contentious take on less significance and agreement will become easier.

Agree On the Things You Can Agree On

There may be a number of things you can agree on at the outset. These might include the goals you have in this situation (to find a solution that will produce a certain result) or your intention in the negotiation (everybody will be able to feel good about what we finally decide to do).

You may be able to easily agree on the financial considerations at play (we have X dollars in the budget or we must leave enough cash reserves to meet unexpected needs).

There may be operational considerations (we must be sure the smooth flow of service to the guests isn't interrupted). Perhaps all parties can agree on the time frame for implementing a solution.

What you agree on at this point is less critical than the fact that you start agreeing on *something*. The climate will improve with each point you can agree on which, in turn, makes further harmony more likely.

Defer Points of Contention

When you run into an area where you can't agree easily, don't dwell on it. "I can see we need to talk about this in more detail. Let's make a note and come back to it later."

Keep in mind that agreement will raise the climate (and the likelihood of success) and disagreement will lower it. Keep the tone

Clean Up the Details

Once you've agreed on everything you can, go back over the list of unresolved items. You may find some that appeared to be sticking points earlier no longer look that way. You can tick them off the list, leaving fewer and fewer issues to be resolved.

Agree on Relative Priorities

Always moving toward what you can agree on, you may be able to agree that one point is more critical than another ("If it means staying within the budget, we can take a little longer to do it.) This will put more items into the "completed" pile and make the task look easier and easier.

Dialogue on Any Unresolved Points

Now you're down to the core issues and it's time for a true dialogue – the free-flowing exchange of ideas. It calls for reflective listening and a sincere willingness to change your position.

This is the time to realize that reaching a workable solution is more important than exactly what that solution looks like. Give up the need to be right in favor of having everybody win.

Give this part of the process as much time as the particular problem deserves. It will take you longer to reach agreement than if you made an executive decision, but the time it will take to implement the solution will be substantially shorter. Reaching consensus will also have a more positive effect on the climate and working environment in the company.

Agree on How You Will Measure Progress

It's easy to overlook this point, but it's important to reach consensus on how you will monitor progress to assure that the agreement you reach is working and what you'll do if things start to get off track.

Be Part of the Solution

Take personal responsibility for the success of the process. You are the role model here as well and others will follow your example.

Be an Advocate for Others

Look for ways that you can help the other parties get what they want from the final resolution.

Be Certain, Not Stubborn

You may have certain non-negotiable standards that figure into the situation but be aware that you can hold to them without being a jerk or making anyone wrong.

Certainty in Action

There's a difference between being stubborn and being certain. Since this is an important point, permit me a brief story to illustrate:

I tend to drive a little fast and in twelve years of living in California, I had occasion to run into the California Highway Patrol once or twice. Their officers are extremely courteous, personable and respectful ... but when you get stopped, there is never a flicker of doubt but that you are going to get a ticket!

Because the thought of talking your way out of it is not even a possibility in the officer's consciousness, it doesn't even cross your mind to attempt it! That's what I mean by certainty.

Professionally speaking, I'm absolutely certain you can't work for me and steal from me, use drugs or have poor sanitation practices. These are like gravity to me.

Because I was certain about these points and didn't even have a thought in my head that they were negotiable, my staff never tried to argue them with me. I would not disrespect other ideas or fail to listen to differing opinions if they were offered, but I would not compromise in these areas and they knew it.

Set a Personal Example

As a final point, always conduct yourself as you want the others in the negotiation to conduct themselves. Listen. Reflect. Be flexible where you can. Ask good questions. Listen and reflect some more. What they see is what you will tend to get.

Disagreements can often be a catalyst for meaningful changes in your organization. Embrace them when they appear, handle them with skill and respect. You and your company will be richer for the experience.

Part 5

Where To
From Here?

"Be different – if you don't have the facts and knowledge required, simply listen. When word gets around that you can listen when others tend to talk, you will be treated as a sage."

– Ed Koch, *former Mayor of NYC*

53
The Daily Question

What Did You Learn from Your Staff Today?
To make a major improvement in your
operation, sit down with your crew one on one
and ask questions like, "What's wrong with this
chicken outfit? What's making your job tough?
If this was your place, what would you change
about it? What can I do to help you be more
successful?" Then shut up and listen.

Your purpose is to foster a human connection
with your crew and gain insight into the way
they think. You don't have to form an opinion
about what they tell you ... nor do you want to.
Your role is just to seek to understand.

What you hear can sound pretty strange at times. For example, somebody
could say, "I think I want to eat my dog." (Take a deep breath and keep
cool!) Odd as it may be, you can entertain that idea and try to understand
why the thought might make sense to them, without having to agree,
disagree or have an opinion one way or the other.

"Interesting," you say, "tell me a little more about that. Hmmm. So you
mean _____. I see. Thanks, that's been very helpful."

**The Perpetual Question I regularly ask subscribers to my weekly
e-letter is, "What did you learn from your staff today?"**

I often pose this question to operators in my seminars and it's worth
bringing up again as a reminder that if you don't have a fresh answer to
this question every day, you're not listening. If you're not listening, you're
not learning. If you're not learning, you're not growing. If you're not
growing, you're toast!

Awhile ago, I asked this question of attendees in one of my seminars.
Their replies might offer a few insights.

First this exchange with Grant Webb, owner of East Side Mario's in Ottawa, Canada. He wrote:

I learned several things:

1) One of my newer but weaker staff is great at suggesting side salads as an add-on at lunch time. I gave her a pat on the back and told her to keep up the good work.

2) I asked my bartender how things were going. She said many of the staff weren't following opening and closing duty lists on the patio and she finds this very frustrating. I told her I understood and I appreciated her feedback.

I'll ask some of the other staff the same question in the next few days. I have a feeling that if I ask if they feel the duties are being done right or not, the work will improve on its own, just due to my interest. The best thing is, no discipline is needed to make this happen.

3) I found out that a new dishwasher I have teaches developmentally challenged kids how to skate.

4) I asked one of my servers why she was a little off and learned she was very hung over. I thanked her for doing her best and asked if she felt a little silly for punishing herself and her guests with inferior service.

5) I had a chat with another staff member about gardening and kid's camps (she has two children). I told her I'd bring some information about a camp I was enrolling my son in.

Thanks for the reminder. I'll try to learn more tomorrow.

I responded:

Great news, Grant! It's amazing what you can learn if you listen. It's amazing what you can get done when you don't try to do it all!

Grant wrote back:

It's amazing what you can learn when you really listen and it's also amazing what you can see when you actually "watch." We often find ourselves caught up in the dynamics of this business and forget what our true roles are.

*My partner Roy and I used to kid each other that we were the highest paid busboys in the city! Not that there's anything wrong in helping out when you're truly needed. The trick is **not** helping out when you're **not** needed. This is something I always knew, but now am finally putting into practice.*

138

I think my staff appreciates my feedback and communication more than my running food for them – especially when they don't need it!

I also heard from Scott Bogart, a CPA in the Los Angeles area who does CFO work for a variety of clients. He wrote:

I really enjoyed your class. Even though your program was designed for the restaurant industry, at least 90% is applicable to all businesses. I'm applying the ideas to all my restaurant and non-restaurant clients.

For one of my non-restaurant clients, I was retained to come in and do CFO work. As it usually happens, I ended up becoming involved in issues that go well beyond the financial arena.

A recent issue involved terminating a Vice President who showed little interest or respect for the thoughts and ideas of her subordinates.

Part of the transition has involved listening to the opinions and creative ideas of the staff she left behind, a staff that up until her departure was sending out resumes because they didn't like coming to work any more.

Before we decided to let her go, we were concerned about the void and how things were going to get done. By moving her out of the way and engaging her staff in dialogue about the tasks at hand, they got excited about coming to work again.

The challenges don't seem very big anymore. It seems like the sun came out and everyone jumped "above the line."

My point in sharing these notes is to underscore that you can tap this incredible source of information just by seeing its value. You don't have to have the answers, you just need to be able to find them ... and one of the most potent things you can do is to listen – really listen – to your staff.

But first you have to drop distractions, clear your head and truly listen. At the very least, sit down with each member of your staff one-on-one and find out who they really are, what they want to be when they grow up and what ideas they have to make your company better.

What did YOU learn from YOUR staff today?

139

54
Fix the System, Not the People

Marvin's Law of Creative Laziness says to "never do any more work than necessary to achieve the results you want." Toward this end, in the interests of your professional survival (and your own sanity), when dealing with daily operating problems I urge you to look for failures in the system, not for failures in people.

Here's an example of a common type of problem that will illustrate what I mean:

Let's say you have an operating standard that calls for evening food orders to be out of the kitchen within fifteen minutes after they're placed.

Note: You determined this standard by observing when the majority of your guests start to become aware of the slow pace of service. By one means or another you have discovered that a ticket time of 15 minutes is what it takes in your operation to meet your guests' needs and expectations during this meal period. I suspect other businesses have similar sorts of standards that are a measure of their success.

Let's also say you have a man named Scott working in the pantry and he's starting to notice that orders often take twenty minutes or more to get out of his station.

Scott is aware that you want the food out in fifteen minutes, so he has two options – he can either keep quiet, hoping you won't notice or he can come to you and report the delays.

If you're the sort of person who sees failures as resulting from the performance of people, you're likely to blame Scott when you learn of the excessive processing times.

If he suspects you're apt to say something like "Thanks for telling me that, Scott. There's obviously a problem here and I think it's you. Since you seem unable to meet our standards, you're fired," you can be sure Scott will never say a word!

Don't laugh, variations on this scene happen all the time.

If you choose to see operating problems as people failures, you virtually guarantee no staffer will ever tell you about a breakdown in the system!

In this environment, few folks will "rat" on their co-workers, They'll figure it's management's job to know what's going on and they don't want to be responsible for someone else losing their job.

Certainly no one will report a problem that may be a result of their own inability to perform if making that report is apt to be professional suicide!

The predictable results are that guest service suffers, operating problems are perpetuated, the "them and us" attitude on the job is validated and your conscientious workers are more likely to become disenchanted. All of this will eventually show up as reduced sales volume, lower morale and increased turnover.

On the other hand, if you were to look at operational breakdowns as failures in the **system**, you would actually encourage people to bring you the "bad news."

With this mindset you would greet Scott's report with enthusiasm and gratitude – enthusiasm because he was taking responsibility for the success of the operation and gratitude because he provided an insight into where the operation might be failing to deliver the desired level of service to your guests.

You might then sit down with Scott to explore where the system might be weak and see what suggestions he has on how to change things to correct the problems.

In this example, there are several possible breakdowns in the system:

- Perhaps the current menu is heavy on pantry items and Scott's station is overloaded.
- Maybe there's an item so complicated to prepare that anytime someone orders it, the entire flow of production jams up.
- Perhaps necessary ingredients are kept in an inconvenient place.
- Perhaps a needed piece of equipment is missing or malfunctioning.

141

- Perhaps orders are garbled when they come in from the dining room because the service staff doesn't understand how to use the new POS system. Every time an order isn't clear, it takes a lot of additional discussion with the service staff to sort it out and get it right.
- Perhaps Scott can't read and has been trying to keep you from finding out.

Even if the problem lies with Scott's inability to perform, it's still a system failure. Was he properly trained? Does he understand what you want him to do? Does he grasp it's importance? If not, you need to re-examine the effectiveness of your training and supervisory systems.

If the standard itself is unreasonable given the labor you have on the schedule, you may need to re-examine your staffing system or reconsider your means of setting standards.

If Scott isn't physically or mentally capable of doing what the position demands or if he is otherwise the wrong person for that particular job, he may be more productive in another position. You need to look for where the job assignment system broke down in allowing him to be assigned to the pantry in the first place.

If Scott is the wrong sort of person to be working in foodservice at all, a problem in your staff selection system allowed him to be hired.

The problem is always in the system, not in the people.

When you look for failures in the system and not for failures in people, it makes it safe for your existing staff to tell you where the snags are.

First of all, they are most likely to know where things aren't working properly. Getting them involved means that the burden of keeping the train on the tracks won't fall entirely on the management. That in itself can be an overwhelming relief!

While it's easy (and tempting) to blame individuals for your operational problems, it's never productive. The difficulty isn't with your people. All they did was ask for a job – you're the one who gave it to them!

This isn't about pointing fingers or assigning blame. If you regard any lapses as your responsibility, you can do something about them. If you always see breakdowns as someone else's fault, you'll continue to be frustrated and perpetuate the same old problems.

142

55
Making it Safe

So how can you move your organization to a point where it feels safe for people to open up and become part of the solution?

If you've been a control-oriented manager who's always placed blame and tried to keep your staff firmly under your thumb, it's going to take time to regain their trust and confidence. It will be difficult but it can be done.

It helps to remember that to do your job properly, you don't need to **have** all the right answers, you just must be able to **find** those answers ... and the deeper in the organization you find them, the more likely they are to "stick."

Here are several qualities and practices that can help establish this dialogue with your staff and start to change things for the better:

Listen to Your Staff, but not just to what they say. Listen for what they mean. Listen with curiosity. Listen for the feelings behind their words. Listen for insights. If you can put your own judgements and opinions on hold, it will help you keep an open mind and help your staff feel better-heard.

If you listen, you'll learn. You might learn something you didn't know. You might get an insight into how another person sees the world. You might pick up an idea that leads to some entirely new growth opportunities for you and the organization.

Consider What They Have to Say because they are closer to most problems than you are and have a different perspective on what's happening. Remember, their observations are just as valid to them as yours are to you. There's incredible wisdom and insight available in your staff if you're courageous enough to place more value on preserving your business than on preserving your ego.

Acknowledge Their Contributions, because what gets rewarded gets repeated. I encourage you to consider rewards after the fact to acknowledge how much you value reports of failures in the system. In my experience, people are eager to become part of the solution when they're acknowledged (with your gratitude if nothing else) for identifying areas that could be working better.

Act on What They Tell You, because nothing validates an opinion more than adopting it. Don't pass up a good idea just because you didn't think of it first. If people see that something will actually happen when they share their ideas, they won't bring you junk.

By eagerly seeking out breakdowns in the system and welcoming any information that points out where the company is falling short of its goals or failing to meet its standards, you become much more approachable and your crew will feel it safe to become part of the solution.

An appreciative, non-judgmental attitude encourages everyone in the company to get involved.

In addition to creating a smoother-running organization, you'll also reduce your workload, foster teamwork and improve job involvement. Your good people will be more inclined to stay and help fix things and less inclined to give up hope or leave out of frustration.

I always found that when I tapped the talent available in my staff, it was easier to spot the real causes underlying our issues. Better yet, it was easier to identify how we might need to change things to make the problem disappear!

The first corollary to Marvin's Law of Creative Laziness is to "never waste time solving a problem you can eliminate!"

56
Dumb as Dirt

We all like to think of ourselves as smart people ... or at least nobody wants to think of themselves as dumb. Let's take a look at each of these possibilities as it relates to dealing with your staff.

"Smart" People
Smart people always figure they have the best answer to a given situation. When a "smart" person asks another's opinion, all the time knowing they already know the "best" answer, the odds are they won't listen to what the other person says anyway.

Did you ever deal with a person like this? What did you think of them? My guess is that they came across as a jerk and looked really stupid to you!

"Dumb" People
In contrast, when you ask someone else's opinion and have no preconceived idea of what you want to hear, it forces you to really listen closely to everything they say.

This can often feel uncomfortable from your perspective, but the person you're dealing with – the one whose ideas you are carefully considering – you look very smart, indeed. It's a natural result of presence and quiet-minded listening.

Presence and a quiet mind are powerful tools when dealing with other people. (It's interesting to note that the less you know, the smarter you look to others ... and the less you know, the more you learn!) A truly smart person realizes there's a wealth of new information available outside of his own experience and seeks to tap into it.

Everything you already know is what got you into the situations you're in. The only thing that will move you ahead is information you don't yet have – and that only comes from new sources and fresh insights.

It's stupid to stay stuck and smart to move ahead ... you figure it out!

57
A Meeting of the Minds

When was the last time you held a really world class staff meeting – I'm talking about a gathering that was so productive and so enjoyable that people left more energized than when they arrived! Did you even realize such a meeting was possible?

If the idea of a truly invigorating staff meeting seems like wishful thinking, you're not alone. The sad fact is most staff meetings ... aren't! In practice, most meetings between staff and management are typically little more than boring sermons.

Worse yet, they're often presented in a distracted, condescending manner that causes the crew shut down their brains and experience a drop in energy. No wonder everybody dreads them!

A truly effective staff meeting is more about reaching a meeting of the minds than simply achieving a gathering of bodies and our old models just don't work anymore.

However, if you come at them in a different way, your staff meetings can help you head off most emergencies before they arise, reduce problems that require your attention, lower staff turnover and create a smoother-running, more profitable operation.

Forget everything you ever knew about staff meetings, think about the relationship between thinking and behavior (Chapter 21) and let's take a fresh look at why we even have such gatherings:

The Primary Objective of Staff Meetings Is to Create a Positive Feeling in the Group

When the feeling in the group is warm and supportive, it's easier to see that we're all in it together, that the success of each individual is inseparable from the success of the entire group.

Absent that good feeling, people will tend to stay focused on their differences. Creating this close feeling is most likely to come from an appreciative sharing of the good news – and there's usually quite a bit when you make a point of looking for it.

Pre-shift meetings aren't the proper time to address individual short-comings – that should be done one-on-one in private – and they're certainly not an appropriate time to dwell on group failings. Dragging out that dirty laundry will drop the mood severely.

The Second Objective Is to Open a Dialogue

A dialogue is a comfortable two-way flow of ideas that leaves all the participants feeling connected and valued. With this sort of rapport, your meetings will naturally tend to instill understanding rather than simply passing along information.

The difference is significant because understanding "sticks" where information is soon forgotten. In addition, the flow of ideas back to management helps eliminate the "them and us" mentality and leads your staff feel that it's also *their* company.

By bringing your crew into the loop, by soliciting, considering and valuing their ideas, staff meetings can help establish and enhance the teamwork in the operation. The likely result is improved customer service, higher productivity and increased profits.

The Third Objective Is Training

A properly conducted staff meeting is a forum for continuous improvement. Even though you have a training program, never miss a chance to pass along a few more hints ... and the pre-shift meeting is the perfect opportunity to do it.

Failure to continuously train can deliver one of two messages: either people are achieving exactly the results you want and can't possibly get any better, or any ninny can instinctively be successful in your company without training.

I doubt either case is true.

58
The Meeting Mindset

When you decide to get serious about staff meetings, it's critical to commit to holding them on a regular basis – ideally before the start of every shift every day – no matter what else is going on.

When pre-shift meetings are sporadic or frequently canceled due to other pressures (and there are **always** other pressures), it shows how you really feel about the value of these meetings. If staff meetings aren't important to you, they certainly won't be important to your crew.

Ideally, pre-shift meetings should last ten or fifteen minutes. Any shorter and you don't have enough time to get anything done; any longer and you may start to lose the crew's attention.

I suggest you pick a specific meeting length and stick with it. I also encourage you to commit to starting and ending your meetings precisely on time – it will show that you take them seriously.

The Internal Element
The factor that most determines whether or not a staff meeting will be effective is the thinking of the person conducting it.

Do you approach your job like a cop, trying to find and correct mistakes or do you define your job as a coach, identifying and building on inherent strengths?

Do you see your staff as bunch of goof-offs looking for a free ride or as intelligent adults who want to make a contribution?

Do you think management must have all the answers or do you view your role as helping your crew discover the answers for themselves?

What you see is what you'll get.

59
Staff Meetings Step by Step

Understanding comes from the inside out rather than from the outside in. When your head is in the right place, you can finally start to conduct energizing staff meetings that will build confidence and get your staff involved in your success.

Now that you understand it's actually possible to hold such meetings, you may be anxious to get started. To get it rolling, here's a suggested format for a 10-15 minute pre-shift meeting:

Good News (1-2 minutes)
The purpose here is to celebrate what's working and set a positive tone for the meeting. Your tone of voice is important as you talk about progress made toward a particular goal, share a success story about one of the staff or read a complimentary letter from a patron.

Everyone likes to hear good news and it helps establish a warm feeling for the rest of the session, particularly when delivered from a feeling of sincere gratitude.

News of the Day (2-3 minutes)
In this segment you might talk briefly about what's coming up on this shift. Mention special promotions in effect and outline anything out of the ordinary that is happening. Be very focused and very brief. If you get lost in this part of the meeting you'll be running the risk of sermonizing and killing the mood.

Staff Feedback (5 minutes)
This is when you open the floor to the crew. To my mind it's the most important part of the meeting because this is when you can start to find out what's on people's minds. The critical skill is to listen without judging the comments you receive.

As an aside, your most valuable information will always come in one-on-one conversations, not in a group. The most likely feedback in a meeting context will concern how various programs are working and topics of concern to everyone in attendance. Defer discussion of any individual issues and deal with them in private.

Avoid any preconceived notions about what people might be saying and be very cautious about injecting your own thoughts into the discussion. This will take practice and discipline, but the results are worth the effort.

Keep in mind that your goal is to create a safe environment for people to share their ideas and to learn from each other. This is where that critical dialogue we discussed really starts.

The quality and quantity of the input you receive will be in direct proportion to how well your staff feels you are listening to what they say – not just **hearing** the words, but understanding the message.

Your willingness to consider their ideas will build trust and over time you'll get more and more involvement from your crew as the level of trust in the organization improves.

At first, you may find people are reluctant to open up in front of their peers. If your initial efforts to get people talking are greeted with silence, here are a few questions that may prompt some discussion:

- Who deserves to be thanked or recognized and for what?
- What is making your job tough?
- What have you noticed that is improving?
- What are we doing that we shouldn't be doing?
- What **aren't** we doing that we **should** be doing?
- What questions came up on your last shift that you couldn't answer?
- If this were your company, what would you change about it?

You get the idea.

As people are talking, give them your undistracted attention. Listen to the **feeling** behind their words. You may want to ask if other people see things the same way as the speaker.

You may want to ask a clarifying question to be sure you understand but resist the urge to add too many of your own comments.

New Information/Training (3-5 minutes)

Every gathering is an opportunity to enhance skills. Particularly in the beginning, if the staff comments segment runs long, shorten the time you allocate to training. It's more important that you learn from the crew than that they learn from you.

Once the team has confidence that there's a forum where *their* ideas will be heard and considered, they'll become more open to receiving new information from you.

Use this part of the meeting to discuss a single point you want the staff to focus on for that shift, to impart product knowledge, to share professional tips or to amplify or supplement material from your regular training program.

Cut to the chase and don't ramble. Your crew will be watching the clock and it is disrespectful to waste their time. You'll build credibility by being direct and finishing on schedule.

More effective staff meetings *are* possible. As your skill and credibility improve, you'll see that pre-shift staff meetings can be an easy way to begin creating a feeling of teamwork in your organization.

The exciting part is that they'll also let you tap the inherent talents of your staff which, in turn, will help the manager's role evolve into one that is more enjoyable and less stressful.

One More Thing

Not everyone on the staff will be able to attend the meeting, of course, so to keep them in the loop, have someone – I suggest it be a supervisor rather than an hourly staff member – take notes of the key points discussed. Following the format I suggested will simplify note-taking.

Put those notes into a loose leaf binder where absent staffers can review what they missed. You may want them to initial that they've seen it. This isn't a perfect system, but it can help avoid communication gaps.

60
Monitor Your Meetings

Now you have some ideas about staff meetings, but are management gatherings any different? The short answer is that the dynamics are the same but the format is usually different.

While facilitating a management retreat for a major resort company, it became apparent to me that they had become addicted to whining. Their meetings typically turned into "gripe sessions" (and not surprisingly, everyone complained about that!)

Perhaps you've experienced something similar in your organization – it's not uncommon. But if this isn't anyone's idea of a good time, why does it happen? More important, what can you do about it? Let's apply the principles we've discussed to the typical management meeting.

It Starts with Thinking
Earlier we discussed two modes of thinking – busy-minded thinking based on what you have in your memory and quiet-minded thinking that comes from tapping into a deeper flow of wisdom.

When people get caught in their own thoughts, the world takes on familiar patterns. The deeper someone gets caught in their own thinking, the lower their mood becomes, the more threatening contrary ideas look to them and the more tightly they hold on to their view of what is "right."

On the other hand, when their minds are relaxed, people are less attached to their own thoughts and can more easily entertain – even relish – the notions of others.

Quiet-minded thinking is the realm of fresh possibilities. When your mind is uncluttered, you'll still have full access to anything in your memory that may be relevant, but you won't be preoccupied with old ideas.

We usually speak of these shifts in your level of thinking as moods. More accurately, they're just a reflection of the extent to which you are attached to your own thoughts at a given moment.

Meetings Have Moods, Too

Like people, meetings have moods, too. There are differing "tones" or feelings in the group which reflect the collective level of states of mind of everyone at the table.

When the tone is high – when the participants' minds are relatively quiet – everybody feels good together. Ideas flow easily, debate is spirited but respectful and the participants feel energized.

When a group is functioning at a high level, time flies. People in the group feel like they're learning new things. They eagerly explore ideas that differ from their own, ask better questions and reflect more on the responses. These are the sort of meetings people look forward to.

As the tone deteriorates – as participants become distracted and more attached to their own thinking – ideas are held more tightly. Dissenting opinions begin to look like personal attacks and the participants will increasingly feel drained of energy.

The Worse it Gets, the Worse it Gets

As a group starts to slide down this slippery slope, agreement becomes more difficult. (As a parallel example, what are the odds you'll be able to successfully resolve anything with your mate when you're both angry?)

The quality of conversation changes. Attitudes of "right" and "wrong" start to appear and the meeting can quickly reach a point where any sort of resolution or agreement is impossible.

If you described the levels of group functioning from higher to lower, it might look like this:

- Feeling like we all see eye to eye ... and beyond!
- Feeling like we are really working together
- Feeling like we are committed to seeing each other's ideas clearly
- Feeling like it is getting hard to get our own ideas across to others
- Feeling bad enough to stop

153

Can you relate to these differences from your own experience of different meetings? If so, you're on your way to being able to do something about it for your own gatherings.

I may develop this idea more in a future book, but for now, just respect the importance of the tone in assuring productivity. Then monitor the tone of your meetings and notice when the feeling and the quality of the conversation starts to change.

The Reasons Aren't Important

It doesn't matter why the group starts slipping into a lower tone, just try to be aware of when it happens. Recognize the symptoms for what they are – merely warning signs, not problems – and use this awareness to help your meetings become more enjoyable.

If you start to notice the quality of discussion taking a downward turn, resist the urge to make any group member wrong for being difficult. I hope by now you understand that assigning blame can only make things worse. If the group starts to gets little off track, just acknowledge the fact and call a recess. Sometimes a short break can help people reset.

If the group can't get back in touch with good feelings, nothing of note is likely to be accomplished, so adjourn the meeting and set a time to get together at a later time. Members of a truly healthy organization might agree as a group that they will discontinue a session if they start to function below a predetermined level.

Management meetings will become easier and more productive as the members of the group deepen their understanding of the relationship between thinking and behavior ... and as lose their tolerance for conflict and ill will.

61
Breaking Old Habits

Now that you hopefully have a different sense of your role as a manager and some ideas of how to achieve more with less effort, all you need to get your life back is to actually reduce the hours you spend on the job!

Long hours are just bad habits. As a recovering independent operator, I know how easy it is to get caught up in the crushing demands of the restaurant. But don't confuse activity with results – more hours typically don't equate to higher productivity. In fact, quite the opposite is true.

Less Is More
Even dedicated managers start to wear down – mentally if not physically – after about 45 hours. As you get more fatigued, you foster a lower work climate which ultimately costs the company money in terms of reduced productivity and irritated patrons.

On the other hand, when you're relaxed and enthusiastic, you tend to promote a more positive feeling on the job.

(It's embarrassing to admit, but during that phase of my career when I was working 120-hour weeks, I knew I wasn't getting the results I should, but I rationalized it by thinking nobody would dare fire me if I was putting in that many hours!)

Once I grasped the relationship between thinking and behavior, I envisioned a formula for management pay where I would pay full wages up to 45 hours a week. After that, because a burned-out manager does more harm than good, I'd start taking money away!

So if you insist on working 70 hours a week, you'll do it for 40% of your base pay. Now *you* figure out what it's going to take for you to go home!

Of course there are busy periods in any business that require more hours on everyone's part (big events, holidays and the like) and the formula isn't intended to penalize anyone for being there during peak times.

Still, there's a big difference between putting in long hours a week before Christmas and regularly working the same schedule week after week.

Although I originally put this together somewhat in jest, I think it has value in nudging workaholics to delegate routine tasks, wean themselves from endless hours and free up enough time to actually have a life!

You need to work your way into this gradually. If you're presently working 60-70 hours a week, it's unrealistic to think you can cut your week back to 45 hours overnight. But you must start somewhere and it helps to have a little structure when changing old habits.

Here's the way it works:

The Formula
There are four levels in the formula, each calling for increased monetary penalties as the number of hours worked increases. This allows you to phase in the structure over time.

For example, you might give managers 90 days to redistribute workloads before you implement Level 1. Three months later, Level 2 can kick in with Level 3 to follow 90 days after that.

Allow another three months before implementing Level 4 and you'll have gradually transitioned yourself (and your managers) into a liveable work week in only a year.

Think of it as a four-step program for recovering workaholics!

If you choose to adopt this idea, discuss it with your managers first and get their buy-in. Make sure everyone understands that the purpose of this structure is to gradually move them toward habits that will help them get their lives back, not to punish them for working extra hours.

MANAGEMENT COMPENSATION FORMULA

HOURS WORKED	LEVEL 1 % of Salary	LEVEL 2 % of Salary	LEVEL 3 % of Salary	LEVEL 4 % of Salary
45	100.0	100.0	100.0	100.0
46	100.0	99.5	99.0	98.5
47	100.0	99.0	98.0	97.0
48	100.0	98.5	97.0	95.5
45	100.0	98.0	96.0	94.0
50	100.0	97.5	95.0	92.5
51	99.5	96.5	93.5	90.5
52	99.0	95.5	92.0	88.5
53	98.5	94.5	90.5	86.5
54	98.0	93.5	89.0	84.5
55	97.5	92.5	87.5	82.5
56	96.5	91.0	85.5	80.0
57	95.5	89.5	83.5	77.5
58	94.5	88.0	81.5	75.0
59	93.5	86.5	79.5	72.5
60	92.5	85.0	77.5	70.0
61	91.0	83.0	75.0	67.0
62	89.5	81.0	72.5	64.0
63	88.0	79.0	70.0	61.0
64	86.5	77.0	67.5	58.0
65	85.0	75.0	65.0	55.0
66	83.0	72.5	62.0	51.5
67	81.0	70.0	59.0	48.0
68	79.0	67.5	56.0	44.5
69	77.0	65.0	53.0	41.0
70	75.0	62.5	50.0	37.5

If you have managers who can't learn how to produce the results you need in an average of 45 hours a week, you don't need them!

157

62
Closing Comments

The ideas in this book may well have raised as many questions as they've answered ... and what I have presented is, in fact, the tip of a much larger iceberg.

This is not information you *learn* as much as it is a set of principles you come to **understand** on deeper levels over time. Even as little as I understood when I arrived at the Olympic Training Center was still enough to make a huge difference in my effectiveness as a manager.

I honestly put in half the time I had ever applied to a job in my life ... and honestly got twice as much accomplished as I ever had in my life. If I'd been willing to work less, I could have gotten more done! Go figure!

Because my understanding of these principles has deepened since then, were I back in the same situation again, I might be able to achieve those results even faster.

Have the Courage to Let it Be Easy
Many restaurant people think of the hours they put in like some sort of badge of honor. "Sixty hours a week? What a wimp! I put in seventy-five, eighty easy." It's madness.

When you respect the power of a quiet mind, when you're willing to know less and listen more, exciting possibilities and insights will appear. You'll look forward to getting to work each day, show up with a smile and the next steps you'll need to take will be obvious.

You'll be amazed how smoothly your life, professionally and personally, starts to unfold. The hardest part is allowing it to be that easy!

The little voice in your head that's been saying, "There HAS to be an easier way to do this"... is right!

I leave you with one of my favorite quotes from Richard Bach, taken from his book, *Illusions.*

A Modern Parable

Once there lived a village of creatures along the bottom of a great crystal river. The current of the river swept silently over them all – young and old, rich and poor, good and evil, the current going its own way, knowing only its own crystal self.

Each creature in its own manner clung tightly to the twigs and rocks of the river bottom, for clinging was their way of life and resisting the current what each had learned from birth.

But one creature said at last, "I am tired of clinging. Though I cannot see it with my eyes, I trust that the current knows where it is going. I shall let go and let it take me where it will. Clinging I shall surely die of boredom."

The other creatures laughed and said, "Fool! Let go and that current you worship will throw you tumbled and smashed across the rocks and you will die quicker than boredom!"

But the one heeded them not, and taking a breath did let go and at once was tumbled and smashed by the current across the rocks. Yet in time, as the creature refused to cling again, the current lifted him free from the bottom and he was bruised and hurt no more.

And the creatures downstream, to whom he was a stranger, cried, "See a miracle! A creature like ourselves, yet he flies! See the Messiah, come to save us all!"

And the one carried in the current said, "I am no more Messiah that you. The river delights to lift us free if only we dare let go. Our true work is this voyage, this adventure."

But they cried the more, "Savior!" all the while clinging to the rocks, and when they looked again he was gone and they were left alone making legends of a Savior.

Fly, my friend!

"The reader will take from my book what he brings to it. The dull witted will get dullness and the brilliant may find things in my book I didn't know were there."
– John Steinbeck, *East of Eden*

Appendix

"The only sure way to succeed is to have access to the experience of others"
— Roy H. Williams, *The Wizard of Ads*

About the Author

Bill Marvin, aka The Restaurant Doctor℠, is a leading authority on how good restaurants can become great. He helps independent operators create organizations that will prosper in tough times and bring out their workers' natural ability to consistently deliver exceptional service and hospitality.

Bill is president of Effortless, Inc., a hospitality research and education company, founder of Prototype Restaurants, and the managing editor of Hospitality Masters Press.

He began his foodservice career washing dishes (by hand!) when he was 14. He's had the keys in his hand, his name on the loans and the payrolls to meet. Bill's hands-on management experience includes restaurants, hotels, clubs and institutions.

He has earned the designation of Certified Speaking Professional from the National Speakers Assn. and is a lifetime member of the Council of Hotel and Restaurant Trainers. Bill was also among the first to be certified as a Foodservice Management Professional by the National Restaurant Assn.

He is a prolific author, a thought-provoking speaker, effective facilitator and a personal coach. His weekly e-letters are received by thousands of independent operators around the world.

His signature project is A Place of Hospitality™, a support/certification system designed to help independent operators become the restaurant of choice by making the experience of true hospitality their competitive point of difference in the market.

For more information, contact Bill Marvin at:

EFFORTLESS, INC.
PO Box 280 • Gig Harbor, WA 98335-0280 USA

(253) 858-9255 or (800) 767-1055
bill@restaurantdoctor.com
www.restaurantdoctor.com

Management Resources
Available at www.RestaurantDoctor.com

RESTAURANT BASICS REVISITED:
Why Guests Don't Come Back and What You Can Do About It
Bill's easy-to-read, common sense look at restaurant service from the guest's point of view. Helps teach the details of good service, develop meaningful middle management training and establish definitive operating guidelines that enhance service. Explores the particular process by which customers form their opinions of restaurant service and provides a competitive advantage for restaurant operators.

GUEST-BASED MARKETING:
How to Increase Sales Without Breaking Your Budget
Bill demonstrates that success doesn't come from beating the competition, but from pleasing your guests. He shows how to work from the inside out to build on your strengths and to use the intrinsic advantages you didn't even know you had. He also suggests dozens of successful, low-cost techniques for mining the most precious resource at your disposal—your existing customer base. (PDF)

FROM TURNOVER TO TEAMWORK:
How to Build and Retain a Guest-Oriented Staff
In this book, Bill Marvin deals with staff turnover, a major cost factor in the hospitality industry. Takes a common-sense approach to why people leave and what can be done about it. Treats such issues as rapport between staff and management, training, salary structure and wages, incentives, performance reviews and disciplinary procedures. (PDF)

CASHING IN ON COMPLAINTS:
Turning Disappointed Diners Into Gold
Nobody likes to get complaints, but if you know how to mine it, there's gold in those gripes! Bill helps you understand what your guests are really worth, the methods to keep your finger on the pulse of your operation and the skills to deal with – and profit from – the complaints you are sure to receive in the normal course of business.

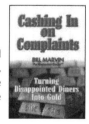

59½ MONEY-MAKING MARKETING IDEAS:
How to Build Volume without Losing Your Shirt
Every restaurateur wants to build sales but nobody has an unlimited advertising budget and most operators have had only limited success with increasing check averages. Bill Marvin explores ways to build volume that are simpler, more effective, much less risky ... and almost free! The secret is to get existing guests to come back more often and say wonderful things about you to their friends.

HOME REMEDIES:
A House Call From the Restaurant Doctor
This is some of The Doc's best stuff. The articles in this book are taken from the first several years of Bill Marvin's "Home Remedies" newsletter. There are some very powerful ideas in here -- some will make you smile, some may irritate you, but all should make you rethink what you "know" ... and that will make all the difference.

50 TIPS TO IMPROVE YOUR TIPS:
The Service Pro's Guide to Delighting Diners
Bill created this pocket-sized paperback as a "bite-sized alternative" to Restaurant Basics. It will help your service staff create more personal connection with your patrons and increase their tips while improving service and guest satisfaction. Quantity prices are available.

50 PROVEN WAYS TO BUILD RESTAURANT SALES & PROFIT
Fifty of the best ideas from the sharpest minds in the business, Featuring Gloria Boileau, Susan Clarke, Barry Cohen, Howard Cutson, Tom Feltenstein, Peter Good, Jim Laube, Bill Main, Phyllis Ann Marshall, Bill Marvin, Rudy Miick and Ron Yudd.

50 PROVEN WAYS TO ENHANCE GUEST SERVICE
This collection takes a look at guest service with profitable ideas from Susan Clarke, Barry Cohen, Howard Cutson, Peter Good, Raymond Goodman, Winston Hall, Jim Laube, Bill Main, Phyllis Ann Marshall, Bill Marvin, Rudy Miick and Banger Smith.

50 PROVEN WAYS TO BUILD MORE PROFITABLE MENUS
This collection explores menus and menu design. This is truly a working books for working people featuring some great money- making secrets from Barry Cohen, Howard Cutson, Peter Good, Raymond Goodman, Jim Laube, Bill Main, Phyllis Ann Marshall, Bill Marvin, Banger Smith and Ron Yudd.

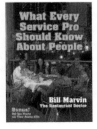

WHAT EVERY SERVICE PRO SHOULD KNOW ABOUT PEOPLE (DVD/CD SET)
In this six-part series, I offer valuable insights that can help your service staff have more fun on the job, be more confident and relaxed when dealing with the public and be more effective at generating income for both the restaurant and themselves! The program goes beyond technique to discuss the principles that are at play in the human interactions you face every day.

PROTOTYPE STAFF MANUAL & HUMAN RESOURCES MANUAL

Originally written for my own account, the Human Resources Manual details the company's policies relating to people. It's information your staff will want to know anyway and failure to have the answers will lower the working climate. The Staff Manual contains all the basic information about the company that every member of the staff needs to be a functioning part of the company culture. (Download)

PROTOTYPE RESTAURANT MANAGEMENT AGREEMENT

Few national hotel companies actually own the properties they manage. Restaurant management contracts are less common but the relationship is the same: an experienced operator takes over a property (often distressed) and attempts to make it profitable. The successful operator retains a percentage of the profits for his efforts and passes the net proceeds through to the owner. (Download)

AUDIO CDS OF LIVE SEMINARS

- How to Prosper in Tough Times
- There's GOT to Be an Easier Way to Run a Restaurant!
- Cashing In On Complaints
- Five Great Ways to Build Sales ... and One Really Lousy One!
- How I Cut My Food Cost by 10% Overnight
- 50 Money-Making Marketing Ideas
- Marketing Advantages of the Independent Operator

... and many more!

ELECTRONIC HOUSE CALL E-LETTER

Since 1997, I have produced a (free!) weekly e-letter where I share what is on my mind at the time. I do not set out to intentionally annoy anyone, but the EHC will always be a means for me to express what I see and what I think it means. You may or may not agree with me, but your agreement -- while reassuring -- it is not required. My purpose is to get you to think in a slightly different way ... or at least become aware of your own preconceived ideas. That is not always comfortable. It can, however, be quite productive.

KEYNOTES AND SEMINARS

Bill's keynotes and seminars focus on the human dimensions of hospitality, customer service, staff selection and retention. He is also in demand as a facilitator for executive retreats. When it comes to dealing with people or managing an organization, if you have ever thought, "There *has* to be an easier way to do this," schedule a house call from the Restaurant Doctor ... even if you're not in the hospitality business!

CONSULTING SERVICES

Bill's active schedule often doesn't leave much time for private consulting, but he's always open to an interesting offer and accepts a few projects a year to keep his skills sharp. His expertise is in the areas of concept refinement and increasing sales, retention and productivity by enhancing the work climate of the company.

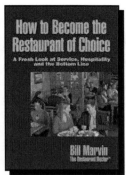

How to Become the Restaurant of Choice

A New Look at Service, Hospitality and the Bottom Line

What is the Restaurant of Choice?

Steve and Nancy Butcher own the modest Nutcracker Family Restaurant in Pataskala, Ohio ... a typical small town diner and gathering spot, seemingly nothing special. One weekend in 2005 they had an electrical fire and the original restaurant burned to the ground.

On Monday morning, their neighbors showed up to help them rebuild. The community simply felt the town wouldn't be the same until they had the Nutcracker back in their lives and took it upon themselves to make that happen. The new restaurant was built ... and Steve was elected town mayor!

Do you think there would be that level of community support if an Applebee's or a McDonald's burned down? More to the point, would YOUR patrons instinctively show up to help rebuild YOUR place if such a tragedy struck? They would if you were truly their Restaurant of Choice.

If you were their Restaurant of Choice, it would mean they think of you as THEIR place. They feel a personal connection to you and your staff. They trust you to always be working in their best interests. They know the names of most of the crew and the staff knows theirs.

They feel comfortable, like old friends when they come in. And even though they are more like family than customers, they know you never take them for granted and consistently work hard to earn their continued patronage.

Becoming the Restaurant of Choice is a high honor to shoot for ... and you can't get there by following a formula or a checklist. It takes a combination of seamless service and personal caring ... hospitality ... delivered in a financially viable manner.

This book is about what it takes to do just that. Written in Bill's conversational style, it is the coming together of many of the ideas he has espoused over his lengthy career as an operator and a perpetual student of the industry.

more information at
www.RestaurantOfChoice.com

167

Re-Thinking Restaurants

WHAT IF we suggested you could actually trigger a **contagious resurgence of hospitality** in your own community by delivering the experience of **heartfelt caring** to every restaurant patron, every time?

WHAT IF we told you we had developed an **elegantly simple system** that provided the logic, methodology and support structure that enabled you to operate with **effortless excellence**?

WHAT IF we assured you and your staff would discover a **fulfilling sense of purpose** and the joyful experience of enriching the lives of the people you serve?

WHAT IF this program was so **irresistible and easily affordable** that hospitality could truly become your competitive point of difference in the market?

Would you think, "These people must be crazy!"
... or would you ask, "How can I become part of this?"

A Place of Hospitality™ is a certification and support program that helps independent restaurateurs ...
- re-discover their roots: hospitality itself!
- enjoy more balance in their lives
- put the joy back into serving the public
- level the playing field when competing against the national chains
- develop a sustainable, steadily growing business built not on discounts and hype but on personal connection and service to the community
- do all this in a way that will be both operationally practical and extremely profitable!

Certification as **A Place of Hospitality** recognizes those independent restaurants who have not only made a deep commitment to provide exceptional personal caring to every guest ... but who have succeeded at it! This certification cannot be purchased and you cannot pay to keep it – you must deliver every day!

learn more at
www.APlaceOfHospitality.com

168

Made in the USA
Charleston, SC
23 February 2016